Costuming
Made Easy
How to Make
Theatrical Costumes
From Cast-off Clothing

Barb Rogers

MERIWETHER PUBLISHING LTD.
Colorado Springs, Colorado

Meriwether Publishing Ltd., Publisher
P.O. Box 7710
Colorado Springs, CO 80933

Editor: Arthur L. Zapel
Editorial coordinators: Amber C. Alexander and Wendy S. Guerrero
Typesetting: Elisabeth Hendricks
Cover and book design: Janice Melvin
Interior illustrations: Janice Melvin
Interior photography: Donna Gordon, Roslyn Hartman, and Barb Rodgers

© Copyright MCMXCIX Meriwether Publishing Ltd.
Printed in the United States of America
First Edition

Library of Congress Cataloging-in-Publication Data

Rogers, Barb, 1947-
    Costuming made easy : how to make theatrical costumes from cast-off clothing / Barb
    Rogers. --1st ed.
         p.   cm.
    ISBN 1-56608-048-7 (pbk.)
    1. Costume. 2. Clothing and dress--Remaking. 3. Vintage clothing. I. Title.
    TT633.R64 1998
    646.4'78--dc21

                                                       98-49796
                                                         CIP

1 2 3 4 5   03 02 01 00 99

Dedication

In loving memory of Jon Luther Lewis,
my son and best friend.

Acknowledgements

A special "thank you" to my wonderful friends and family that helped make this project possible. Your love, support, and help has been greatly appreciated.

Tom & Jacqui McKibben, Mattoon, Illinois, Christopher Brown, Sun City, Arizona, Dimetrius Vonglis, Sun City, Arizona, David Tibbits, Plymouth, Massachusetts, Susan Rodgers, Plymouth, Massachusetts, Stephan Hollenbeck, Indianapolis, Indiana, Bambi Krajek, West Salem, Illinois.

And to my husband, Junior, who was by my side throughout, dressing mannequins, running my errands, and putting up with me when no one else would have. All my love.

Contents

Chapter 4

Introduction

Is sewing a lost art? Not yet, but it seems to be moving in that direction. Since clothing can be bought more cheaply than made these days, what is the point? Many young women have never sewn on a button or put a hem in a skirt. Budgets for the arts have been cut severely in the last few years. So, what do you do with a class of non-seamstresses, very little money, and a play to put on?

Step back from your machine, file your patterns away, and forget everything you know about conventional sewing. I am going to take you into the fascinating world of conversion costuming.

They say that "necessity is the mother of invention." And in my case, it was the birth of my career as a costumer. As a young, single mother with children who wanted things I couldn't afford, I learned to improvise with what I had at home or could find in a thrift shop. I realized early in life that I had a flair for making something from nothing, and in particular, costumes.

Throughout the years, I made costumes for extra money. I had no idea how to sew, didn't own a machine, but could come up with beautiful, prize-winning costumes... and loved doing it. It became my dream to one day open my own costume rental shop.

I realized that dream the year I turned thirty-eight. I was returning from a job interview to become a probation officer when my husband asked me why I wasn't excited about it. After all, that was why I went to college. I explained to him what the job would entail. He asked me if I could do anything I wanted, what would it be? I shared my dream.

Upstairs, over two bars we owned, were fifteen rooms that had been old apartments years before and had been used for storage since. Still without a sewing machine or any formal knowledge of sewing, I began making costumes at home and cleaning up one of the rooms over the bar to use as a shop. The excitement built.

By the first of October, 1985, Broadway Bazaar Costumes

opened with 130 costumes. As a gift, my best friends bought me an old treadle sewing machine at an auction—you know, one of those you pump up and down. I still use that sewing machine to make my costumes today.

As I filled one room with costumes, I would fix up another, until all fifteen were full. I began theatrical costuming during my third year. It is a whole new world of costuming. People like me didn't go to the theatre. I was lucky if I had time to sit through a whole show on television. But I was teachable, and I learned. I scoured the library, rented videos, and picked up what I could from others who were more educated about theatrical costumes. I found I could do theatrical costumes the same way I did others; I just had to be more selective about the used clothing I bought.

This book is dedicated to all of you who have to do costumes for a production with no knowledge of sewing, not much time, and a limited budget. I will show you, in a simple and cheap way, how to come up with the same results and have fun doing it. You must be willing to put away your old ideas, to scour thrift shops, rummage sales, or anyplace else that you might find useful garments. You must be willing to do research at the libraries, listen to people who know more than you do, and even watch the same video over and over until the costumes are planted in your mind.

I've chosen some of the most commonly done stage plays and built the costumes for the main characters and some of the minor players, using my conversion method. I will share with you, through pictures and diagrams, how to accomplish the same results. It is easier, cheaper, and time-saving. The most expensive costume I made cost under thirty dollars, and most cost much less. That is less than the rental price for one day's use in most rental shops. If you have found a garment that fits your actor, there is no need for time spent to measure and do fittings. The basic garment is made so you don't have to do that. In many cases, the conversion takes less than twenty minutes unless you are using fabric paint or need to dye the garment. Any costume accessories that I didn't make are contained in the reference section with instructions on where to obtain them.

If you follow my lead, I know you will be pleased with the results. The one thing that you must always remember is to "never sew if you don't have to."

Materials

You might be saying to yourself, "I can't do this," but if you can read a book, push a needle through fabric, and glue things together, you can do conversion costuming.

All materials used in this book are easily accessible and reasonable to purchase. You should be able to find whatever garment you will be using at a thrift shop, a discount store, from your closet, or perhaps, your mother's closet. Wherever you locate your garment, make sure it fits the person comfortably and has the potential to become the costume you desire. Research the style and pick something as close as possible.

Needles and Thread

Since we are not professional seamstresses, we will be using black thread for dark fabrics and a light beige or white for lighter materials. Occasionally, I have used white thread on black fabric and colored it with a magic marker—the world didn't come to an end. I use whatever I have on hand that will work. There are no rules to conversion costuming.

You will need a couple of needles. Since we will be doing as little sewing as possible, keep one handy and another one in case you lose the first. I keep a leather needle in my treadle machine. It will sew through almost anything. They make them for all types of machines.

Most of the sewing in this book will be in the form of tacking, sewing two pieces of fabric together in a straight line, and hemming.

Scissors and Glue

A good pair of sharp, pointed scissors is a must. Your scissors will be in constant use.

Glue is the most important ingredient in conversion costuming. My first glue gun was a "hot" glue gun. This gun will remove three layers of skin with one touch. I used one for several years and am not sure to this day if I have any fingerprints left. **TIP:** If you get hot glue on your finger, don't put it in your mouth.

With the introduction of the new Magic Melt glue gun, I found the answer to my prayers. The glue dries faster, it holds as well as hot glue, and you can still wash your garment; plus, it only burns off the top layer of skin. This gun is my preference.

Gluing is easier and faster than sewing, and it holds better than thread in some instances. In this book, when I say I glued something I mean that I used a Magic Melt glue gun and glue. See the reference section for the adhesive company where you can purchase the gun and glue if you can't find one in a fabric shop or department store near you.

To Dye or Not to Dye

I had never dyed fabric before I started my business. I had several really wonderful gowns in my shop that wouldn't rent because they were white and customers said they looked too much like wedding gowns. What to do? Dye them? How hard could it be? My first dye job was a disaster and ended up as a gown for Frankenstein's bride, because I didn't read the instructions. I now know to wash the garment in cold water, remove it, leaving it wet, and then set my machine on the hottest water and the longest cycle. Dissolve the dye, add salt to the water and when the machine begins to agitate, add the garment. Sometimes I have to run the garment through the first cycle two or three times if I want a more brilliant color. The garment can be dried in the dryer on a low setting. To clean your machine, set the water level on the highest setting, add detergent and a cup of bleach and let it complete the cycle. An old towel run through the dryer will remove any dye residue.

Dye opened up a whole new world for me. I found that I could mix colors and come up with some interesting shades. Gowns that were soiled to the point of no return could be dyed, erasing the soiled areas. So, if you have found the perfect garment for your costume, but it is the wrong color or soiled... dye.

Pins

Never sew when a pin will work as well or better. I buy big bags of safety pins in assorted sizes for a number of uses. If I use a pin inside the garment that will be next to the skin, I shoot some glue over it and cover it with a piece of felt, fabric or foam. When a pin is used to hold up a section of the garment, I glue on a flower, a piece of jewelry, or fabric to cover it. Pins are fine but must be covered and safe.

Trim

I cannot tell you how many times I have rummaged through last year's Christmas decorations or old flower arrangements to find trim for a costume or hat. I buy old hats with feathers and flowers, dresses just for the buttons, and shawls for the fringe. I pick up old jewelry at rummage sales, auctions, and thrift stores when it's cheap. I watch for half-price sales at the fabric stores and offer to buy their "ends" box. (That's a box they keep under the counter to toss the ends in when there isn't enough to sell.) I can pick up a lot of trim for very little money.

Fabric Paint

I used to spend countless evening hours sewing sequins and beads on costumes, until I discovered fabric paint. In a short time, I can do what appears to be an entire beaded eagle on an Native American costume, bring glitter beads to a gown, write words on a jacket, etc., by using fabric paint. It is wonderful, washable, cheap, and easy to use.

Buttons can be a problem. Sometimes I can't find what I need, the color is wrong, or I need a more antique look. Fabric paint to the rescue. I can make the buttons out of the paint, cover buttons with it, or decorate buttons for an older look.

Rhinestones and other heavier trims have a tendency to pull loose after a few washings. If I use intermittent drops of fabric paint along the trim it helps hold them on longer.

Glitter fabric paint has replaced a lot of the sequins and beads I used in the beginning. Sometimes I draw my design on before I begin painting.

If I have a stand-up collar that needs to stay stiff, fabric paint saves me again. The paint will help hold it up and continues to do so even after being laundered.

Never place any costume utilizing glue and fabric paint in hot water or a hot dryer. Wash garments in cold water and hang them to dry.

Theatrical
Costumes
Chapter 1

Annie

While we are not concerned with the plot of the story, we are interested in the setting, time period, and the type of clothing worn. *Annie* is set in New York City, 1933, during the Great Depression. There are still many people out of work and living on the streets, wearing rags. Annie is living in a very poor orphanage, run by Mrs. Hannigan, who is certainly a common soul. The woman has no taste and treats the children poorly.

Many of the costumes used for this play can be found in thrift shops. I have picked the ones you might need to search for or design by conversion. **Mrs. Hannigan's** flowered dress, trimmed in lace is a commonly sought-out costume and a good place to start. The original garment was a flowered dress with split leg pants. I loved the fabric because it would not fray and it had the colors I desired. I located a red crinoline slip to put under the dress. The hat was a black pill box enhanced with black netting and a red bow. See Mrs. Hannigan #1.

Mrs. Hannigan #1

Making the Costume

1. Cut the inseam from the legs.
2. Sew the legs together to form a skirt, leaving the front split.
3. Cut off the bottom to the length desired and hem.
4. Using the already hemmed bottom of the dress, cut two sections off to make a flounce around the end of the sleeves.

Glue red lace inside the flounce and glue the flounce to the cuff. Glue trim around the edge to cover where it is attached.

5. Glue red lace trim at neckline and around the inside edge of the skirt.

6. Add red underskirt, black pill box hat with added netting and a red lace bow, and dark hose and shoes. Add gaudy jewelry.

Mrs. Hannigan #1
Original Garment

Add red lace.

Add large ruffle from hem material.

Add red lace.

Cut

Red underskirt under dress

Mrs. Hannigan has one scene where she tries to seduce Daddy Warbucks. She will need to be dressed as a 1933 floozy. I couldn't find the type of dressing gown I needed, so I converted a dress into a robe and added a short black slip under it for the effect. See Mrs. Hannigan # 2.

Making the Costume

1. Turn the dress around to the back.
2. Cut straight up the center, eliminating the zipper as you go.
3. Glue down the edges where you cut. Remove the chiffon roses from the bodice.
4. Glue ostrich feathers (can substitute a boa if you can't find ostrich feathers) to the neck and front of the bodice.
5. Add short black slip, dark thigh high stockings, beads, and high heel shoes. I glued two of the chiffon roses on the toes of her shoes.

Mrs. Hannigan #2

Back View

Cut down back seam. Remove zipper.

Add feather trim.

Glue edge back.

Glue edge back.

Mrs. Hannigan #2
Original Garment

You might think the costume will look funny from the back, but it hangs well and you can't tell it was a dress. Trust me, it will look great on stage.

Have fun with Mrs. Hannigan, but remember that she will need to move and dance in her costumes. Allow plenty of room for movement. Her accessories are important for the total effect.

Grace #1

Grace is Daddy Warbucks' secretary and "gal Friday." She first appears at the orphanage in a man's tailored suit with a woman's fedora: very conservative. Her skirt was mid-length and I could not find one in a style I considered suitable. I did find a pant suit that would work. See what you think. See Grace #1.

Making the Costume

1. Dye the suit with one package of black dye, allowing it one cycle. It comes out a nice grey.
2. Cut the inseam out of the pants, sew legs together to form a skirt, and hem at the length desired.
3. Sew in two pieces of elastic at waist directly under the arms to give the jacket a more tailored look.
4. Add dark hose, black shoes, a black tie at the neck, and a rather plain, long-sleeved white blouse. I used a woman's black fedora hat with a grey hatband to finish the look.

Grace #1
Original Garment

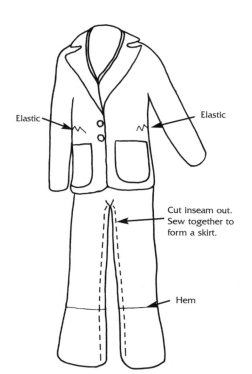

Elastic

Elastic

Cut inseam out. Sew together to form a skirt.

Hem

Later, Grace wears a summer dress. It should be a chiffon dress that moves well while she dances. I bought a dress that was the style I wanted, but the wrong color and too long. See Grace #2.

Grace #2

Making the Costume

1. Dye the dress with gold dye.
2. Cut off the bottom ruffle of the underdress and hem.
3. Use the bottom ruffle to make the flowing neck scarf that matches the dress.

Cut off bottom of underdress.

Cut off hem — use for scarf.

Grace #2
Original Garment

Grace #3

For the final scene, when Grace has caught her man (Daddy Warbucks), she wears white evening wear. I converted a long white dress into a jacket and skirt, and enhanced it with white sequins. See Grace #3.

Making the Costume

1. Just below the first button under the waist, cut across the dress, angling the cut so the back is longer than the front.
2. Cut off collar and down neckline to form a V-neck. Glue sequins around edges where you cut. You will not need to hem because you are gluing trim on—it will seal the edges. Add sequin trim to arms and front of jacket for design.
3. Trim off top of skirt and glue down waist above top button. If the waist is too big, glue together spots in the back to make it smaller. It won't show because the jacket will cover it. Glue sequin trim on skirt.
4. Add white shoes and whatever jewelry you desire.

Grace #3
Original Garment

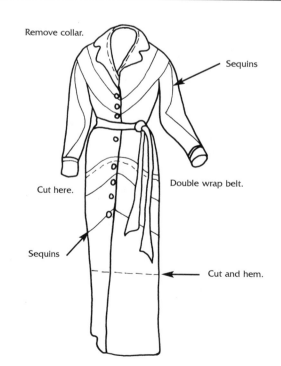

Remove collar.

Sequins

Cut here.

Double wrap belt.

Sequins

Cut and hem.

Annie #1

Daddy Warbucks #1

Two costumes come to mind when I think of **Daddy Warbucks.** He wears a double-breasted suit with a white shirt and tie. At the end of the play he is in a shawl-collared white tux jacket with black pants. The key words you need to remember here are wealth and businesslike.

I was lucky enough to find an elegant men's double-breasted suit at an antique store. Even though I paid twenty dollars for it, I considered it a bargain. It was exactly what I was looking for. If you have trouble finding a double-breasted suit, see the section on *Guys and Dolls* (page 44) where I show you how to convert a regular suit into a double-breasted suit.

I added a white shirt, dark tie, and a man's period hat. Period hats are more difficult to find or make for men. See the reference section at the back of the book to see where you can buy them wholesale.

Daddy Warbucks #2

By changing the tie and jacket, removing the hat, and adding a dark cummerbund, you will have the costume for the final scene. See Daddy Warbucks #1 and #2.

Annie's costumes are easy. She starts out in old sleepwear, changes into a ragged dress, apron, and sweater, and later into nicer dresses after she has gone to live with Daddy Warbucks. The dress I think of most often is the red dress with a white collar, cuffs, and belt. I bought Annie's dress at a rummage sale, hemmed it and added a white belt. See Annie #1.

East Indian Manservant

The mystery of the Far East surrounds the **East Indian Manservant.** I bought a white lab coat for his tunic, and white pants. I made a white turban of non-fray fabric, which I wrapped and glued around the dome of an old hat. The sash is the hem of a full skirt. It should be colorful. For design on the jacket and turban, I used drops of fabric paint. A scarf around the neck finished the costume.

If your lab coat has an embroidered name, as many of them do, simply glue a piece of fabric over it or cover it with fabric paint.

East Indian Manservant
Original Garment

Lily Costume

The same lab coat and white pants can be dyed navy blue, with a dark belt, a hat, and a badge to make a period policeman costume which you will also need for the play. See East Indian Manservant Costume.

The original garment for **Lily's** dress was a thin, black fabric with white triangles. I ran the dress through one cycle of the washer with red dye to make it more colorful. I added a black satin slip, jewelry, black strapped high heels, a belt, and a small black pillbox hat which I garnished with feathers, flowers, and black netting. Add an old coat, hat, and wig for her disguise. See Lily Costume.

Rooster is a 1930s con man. He should be dressed like a gangster from that period. I used a double-breasted jacket, pants, a striped shirt and a bow tie. Add an overcoat and old felt hat for Rooster's disguise. See Rooster Costume.

If you want a more serious gangster look for Rooster, see the section on *Guys and Dolls.*

I found a wonderful pink silky suit I thought would make a great costume for one of the **Boylan Sisters.**
When I put it on the mannequin, I realized the skirt was too short for the period and it had a small hem so I couldn't let it out. What to do? I cut the elastic top off the skirt, sewed the remaining skirt onto the top section of an elastic waist white slip, and achieved the length I wanted. You can do that if the jacket is long enough to cover it and the actor doesn't have to go without the jacket. I added a ruffled white blouse and jewelry.

For the Boylan sister's hat, I used an old, wide-brimmed, straw hat with a rounded dome. I cut the brim down and glued on white and pink flowered material. Then I embellished it with netting, feathers, and flowers. See Boylan Costume.

Lily Costume
Original Garment

Rooster

Boylan Costume

For **FDR**, you can use a grey or brown pinstriped, double-breasted suit with a white shirt, tie, and hat from the period. Again, if you have trouble locating a double-breasted suit, see the section on *Guys and Dolls* (page 44) to see how to convert a regular suit to a double-breasted suit.

You will need maids, policemen, a cook, a butler, townspeople, and others for your production. I hope my examples have shown you how to convert your way to a wonderful production of *Annie*.

Annie Get Your Gun

When you think of **Annie Oakley**, you probably think of her in a two-piece, fringed western costume, rifle at the ready. Since there will be other chapters to show you how to make dresses and gowns, I chose a shooting outfit for this chapter.

The white vest and skirt were purchased at a thrift shop. I found the hat and blouse at a rummage sale. The boots belonged to a friend who no longer needed them. See Annie Oakley Costume.

If you can't find any toy guns, see the reference section of this book.

**Annie Oakley
Costume**

Annie Oakley
Original Garments

Making the Costume

1. Cut the vest shorter, angling longer in the back.
2. Glue fringe and sequins around the edge of the vest and the skirt hem.
3. Decorate skirt, vest, and hat with fabric paint.
4. To fringe the boots, apply sticky-back loop and eye tape to the boot tops and sew loop and eye tape to the fringe. That way, no matter how many shooting costumes you use, you can change the color of the fringe and have a pair of matching boots.

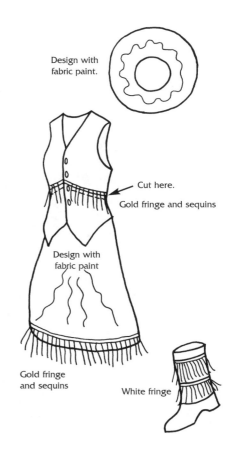

Design with fabric paint.

Cut here.
Gold fringe and sequins

Design with fabric paint

Gold fringe and sequins

White fringe

**Buffalo Bill
Costume**

Buffalo Bill, Pawnee Bill, and Frank Butler all wear long coats for this play. Long coats can be difficult to find. When I need one, I usually look for a doctor's lab coat. They are white, as a rule, and they dye well. I've chosen Buffalo Bill because he is so striking and handsome in his long fringed jacket and high top boots. The same type of design can be used for the other players.

Suedecloth makes great fringe. I found a dress at a yard sale that would work well. It was not the color I wanted, but I knew I could dye it. See Buffalo Bill Costume.

Gloves with large fringed cuffs can be added to this costume. In the sketch, you will see how to make them.

You will normally use tan pants, a white or tan shirt, a string tie, and western-style hat for these costumes. Since I live in Arizona, cowboy hats are easy to find at sales, but if they are not available to you, see the reference section for a place to buy them.

Buffalo Bill
Original Garment

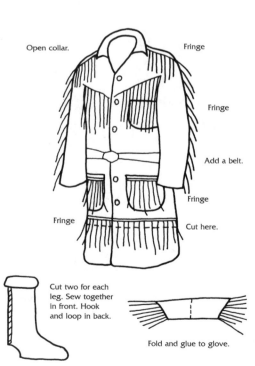

Open collar.

Fringe

Fringe

Add a belt.

Fringe

Fringe

Cut here.

Cut two for each leg. Sew together in front. Hook and loop in back.

Fold and glue to glove.

Making the Costume

1. Dye the lab coat and suedecloth dress with brown dye.
2. Cut off strips of the dress and glue them to the lab coat and pants where you want fringe. Fringe the fabric.
3. For a Native American bead look, use drops of fabric paint where you glued fringe to the coat.
4. Make a hatband from the suedecloth and use fabric paint for design to match the coat.
5. The tie belt is strips of fabric braided together.
6. Add boot tops and gloves. Boot tops are very easy to make from leather-like fabrics. If you don't wish to make them, they can be bought through several wholesale companies. See reference section.

Any good Western has to have a saloon and girls in satin, sequin, and feathered **Dance Hall Dresses**. They are easy and fun to make. I think we must all have a side of us that wants to be daring, and these costumes represent that side.

I've chosen two styles of dance hall dresses because some women like to show their upper body and others their legs. I'll also show you a way to look sexy and show very little.

The zipper was broken in the long, red, satin dress, so it was cheap. As you have probably figured out, I don't do zippers. To restore the dress to use, I bought metal hooks and eyes already sewn on twill tape and sewed it into the back. It worked well and was much easier to deal with. See Dance Hall Costume #1.

Remember that the pins should be covered with glue so they won't show or stick the individual.

I told you I would tell you a way to be sexy and modest at the same time. With this dress, don't cut out the center of the chest, and add a long black satin skirt.

Dance Hall Costume #1

Dance Hall Costume #1
Back View

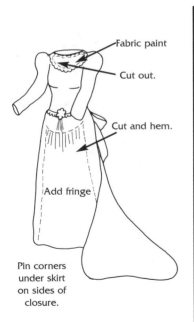

Fabric paint

Cut out.

Cut and hem.

Add fringe

Pin corners under skirt on sides of closure.

Making the Costume

1. Dab black fabric paint for design on the chest. Let dry. Cut the fabric away from the center.
2. Glue a piece of fringe and a flower at the throat.
3. Cut skirt front and hem.
4. Glue on black fringe, red ruffle, and one silk flower at the waist.
5. In the back, cut the train in half. Glue the lower half of train under the upper half, directly to the dress.

Dance Hall Dress
Original Garment

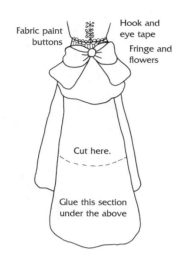

Fabric paint
buttons

Hook and
eye tape

Fringe and
flowers

Cut here.

Glue this section
under the above

6. Using safety pins, pull up the corners of the top layer, and pin them at the waist on either side of your hook and eye tape, from underneath.
7. Glue on large bow for that dance hall look.
8. Glue fringe and flowers at sides of back to cover where you have pinned.
9. Up the back, make small buttons on both sides of the hook and eye tape with black fabric paint.
10. Glue feathers to a headband for the headpiece. Add a boa.

The teal-colored prom dress was given to me. It had good stiff boning and a wonderful fitted waist that would work well for a dance hall dress, with very little work. See Dance Hall Costume #2.

The headpiece is a black, fabric-covered headband with feathers and sequins glued to it. Please check the reference section for places to purchase feather boas.

Fishnet pantyhose may be worn with dance hall dresses, and for shoes you can use any type of high heels. If you are going with the shorter skirt, a garter may be added.

**Dance Hall
Costume #2**

**Dance Hall
Costume #2**
Back view

Making the Costume

1. Remove the skirt and bow from the dress.
2. Trim off the upper part of the skirt, leaving about an inch above the gathers.
3. Use a skirt cut off from another dress, and glue it to the front outside hem of the bodice. Glue wide sequins over it to seal and hide the edge.
4. Form a waistband from the inch you left on the back skirt and glue it together. Pin it to the back and sides of the dress.

Dance Hall Costume #2
Original Garment

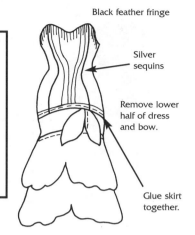

Black feather fringe

Silver sequins

Remove lower half of dress and bow.

Glue skirt together.

5. Glue sides of short black skirt inside the back flounce.
6. Glue the large bow on the back to cover the pins and add sequin trim.
7. Decorate the bodice with glued-on sequins. I used feathers for the trim on the bodice top.

Almost any brown dress with no waist can be made into a **Native American** costume. You don't have to have suede or leather. From a distance, almost any fabric will work.

I have included two samples of Native American costumes for women and a man's fringed scout costume.

Native American #1

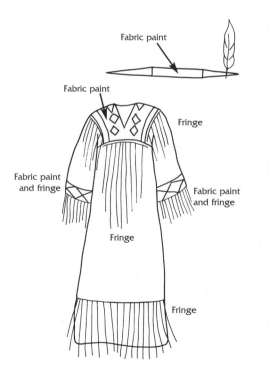

Fabric paint

Fabric paint

Fabric paint

Fringe

Fabric paint and fringe

Fabric paint and fringe

Fringe

Fringe

Fringe

Making the Costume

1. The original garment is a brown cotton, smocked dress with sleeves.
2. Using an old suedecloth dress, cut strips from it and glue them where you want fringe.
3. Using fabric paint drops, make Native American bead designs at the bodice and sleeves.
4. A strip of suedecloth can be used for the headband — bead with fabric paint and add a feather.

Native American #1
Original Garment

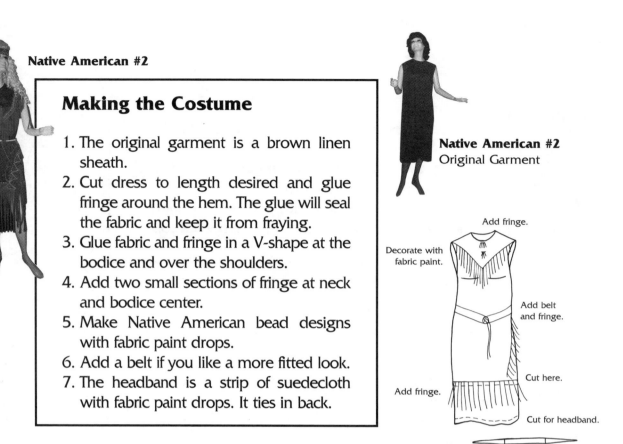

Native American #2

Making the Costume

1. The original garment is a brown linen sheath.
2. Cut dress to length desired and glue fringe around the hem. The glue will seal the fabric and keep it from fraying.
3. Glue fabric and fringe in a V-shape at the bodice and over the shoulders.
4. Add two small sections of fringe at neck and bodice center.
5. Make Native American bead designs with fabric paint drops.
6. Add a belt if you like a more fitted look.
7. The headband is a strip of suedecloth with fabric paint drops. It ties in back.

Native American #2
Original Garment

Add fringe.

Decorate with fabric paint.

Add belt and fringe.

Cut here.

Add fringe.

Cut for headband.

The clothing and design for the **Fringed Scout** can be used to make Native American male costumes also.

Fringed Scout

Making the Costume

1. Find some tan pants and a long square tailored shirt. Dye them brown. Remove the collar of the shirt.
2. Cut up a leather skirt for the fringe. Put the underside face out for a leathery look
3. Glue strips of skirt down the leg seams, on the back of the arms, across the shoulders, around the neck, and over the pockets. Cut into fringe.
4. Add a black belt.

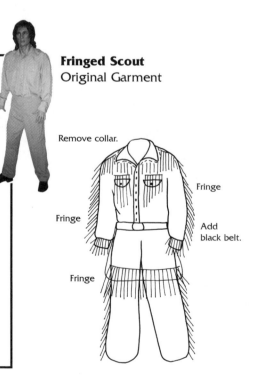

Fringed Scout
Original Garment

Remove collar.

Fringe

Fringe

Add black belt.

Fringe

I was fortunate to find an old prom dress which was perfect for a **Town Woman** from the era. It had mid-length puffed sleeves, a long skirt with a shorter, gathered overskirt, a little lace and ribbon on the front, and lace trim around the overskirt. When you dye a dress such as this, the lace and ribbons tend to dye darker than the body of the dress. I like the look. See Town Woman Costume.

Making the Costume

1. Dye the dress blue.
2. Bring overskirt up one side and pin. Glue flowers over the area where you pinned.
3. Add a white silk rose at bodice center. Add a crinoline for fullness.
4. The hat is a straw hat with the sides glued up and feathers and flowers glued on. The choker is a piece of rippled string sequins.
5. You could add a pair of short white gloves and a parasol if desired.

Town Woman Costume

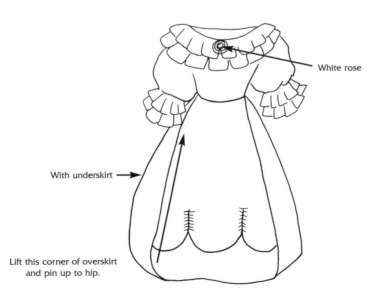

White rose

With underskirt →

Lift this corner of overskirt
and pin up to hip.

Town Woman
Original Garment

Town Man #1

All types of people inhabit a community. You will need to be able to represent many of them so they are distinguishable from each other, oftentimes with only a few costumes. You know what a regular cowboy looks like so we won't have to go into that, but if you want more specific characters, see **Town Man #1 and #2.**

He could be the grocer, the telegraph operator, the hotel clerk, or even the piano player in the saloon. He could wear black and grey pinstriped pants, white shirt, black vest, black string tie, arm garters, and a derby. Put it together and add a watch chain.

If you need cutaway coats, see the section on *Hello Dolly* (page 56) for easy conversions of several different types of men's coats. For men's hats, see the reference section at the back of the book.

By merely adding a jacket, a different hat and wig, and a walking stick, you have a distinctly different character.

Town Man #2

Camelot

Regal, flowing gowns with jeweled collars, capes, and crowns are the dress of the day for **Guenevere**. I have found that old wedding dresses do well for her. I found two wedding gowns that could be bought for under twenty dollars each at the thrift shops. With all the weddings and divorces going on today, it is not as difficult as you might think to find reasonably priced wedding gowns at yard sales, thrift shops, and even in the trash. That's a stretch, but I did find one years ago in a trash bin.

A woman's white and gold jacket became the collar of her queenly attire. See Guenevere Costume #1.

Guenevere Costume #1

Making the Costume

1. Dye the wedding dress blue.
2. Cut cuffs off and split sleeves up to the elbows.
3. Glue gold trim around split sleeves and bodice front.
4. Remove collar from jacket. Sew hook and loop tape to ends to fasten in back of dress. Glue collar to dress just below the bust. Glue gold trim to it.

Guenevere #1
Original Garment

Guenevere #1
Original Garment

5. Cut a circle out of the white and gold jacket, leaving shoulders in, to make the regal collar. Glue on gold trim and use fabric paint for jewels.
6. Glue red fabric cape to inside of shoulders and back neck of collar. Hem the bottom.
7. Using an old hat brim, cover with red fabric and gold trim, then add wired gold trim for the top of the crown.
8. Add a long-sleeved white blouse with ruffles at the cuffs and a crinoline to add fullness to the skirt.

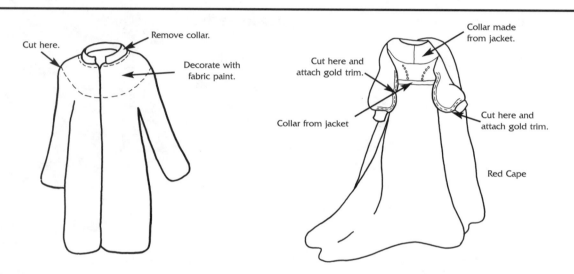

If you have a problem finding crinolines at thrift shops or yard sales, see the reference section for places to buy them wholesale.

In one well-known scene, Guenevere is in the park near Camelot and she is singing and dancing with a group. My second wedding dress was used for that costume. See Guenevere Costume #2.

Gueneverе Costume #2

Making the Costume

1. Carefully cut off the sheer outer skirt. You will be using it later so don't dye it. Dye the remainder of the dress, including the separate train, with dark blue dye.
2. Remove sleeves up to the trim at upper arms.
3. Cut out neckline.
4. Split the train lengthwise and cut off at the top.

Guenevere #2
Original Garment

5. Glue down all raw edges and trim with sequins.
6. Glue half of train to each sleeve.
7. Using silk flowers and sequins, glue bouquets of flowers on the front of the skirt.
8. Add flowers at the neckline and a small flowered wreath for the head. I used part of a bridal veil.
9. Long, white gloves may be added.

Sequin trim

Cut here.

Cut off sleeves.

Cut train in half.

Cut here.

Cut off sheer outer skirt.

Glue to sleeves.

Silk flowers and sequins

Sequin trim

**Arthur
Costume #1**

Where in the world do you find gold armor for **King Arthur**? If you can't find it, can you make it? Yes! If you have a costume shop in your area, you can buy cheap plastic armor and helmets. If not, see the reference section of this book for a place to buy it. It is flimsy, breaks easy, and doesn't look very good, but I can show you how to make it work for you — and Arthur.

I purchased a woman's extra large dress to use for my tunic. See Arthur Costume #1.

Because the helmet I had was a Roman armor helmet, I had to make some changes. Before I coated or covered it with fabric, I had to remove the brush from the top and add a piece at the jaw made of foam.

When covering with sculpt or coat, the plastic will be flexible and last for a long time. All in all, I was pleased with the look.

Making the Costume

1. Buy a plastic breastplate, leg covers, and helmet. Coat them with sculpt or coat (see reference section).
2. While coating is still wet, press gold lame fabric into it, leaving extra fabric around the edges. Let dry overnight.
3. Glue edges down inside the armor.
4. Put another coat of sculpt or coat on the fabric and let it dry.
5. Fasten front and back of breastplate together with sections cut out of a leather belt.
6. Decorate with fabric paint and glue to shoulders of breastplate.
7. Use a large black dress for the tunic. Cut the sleeves out, leaving extra space in the armholes to accommodate a man.
8. Cut off the bottom of the dress to desired length.
9. Glue trim around bottom and armholes.
10. Find a long-sleeved red shirt — turn it backwards.
11. Remove the regular collar and cut a collar out of the top of the red shirt.
12. Cut cuffs off and use the lower sleeve for arm bands. Decorate the arm bands and collar with fabric and fabric paint. If you glue fabric on, go around the edge with fabric paint to make it look better, stay on longer, and keep from fraying.
13. Add tights, a long-sleeved black shirt, and a sword.

Arthur #1
Original Garment

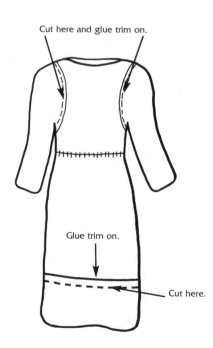

Cut here and glue trim on.

Glue trim on.

Cut here.

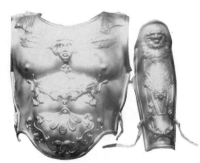

**Original Plastic Armor
for Arthur #1**

The king can't run around in armor all the time, so I have made another costume to use as an example of what he and other knights might wear around the castle.

A green dress with an elastic waist and a red dress with no waist, both extra large, will make up the body of Arthur's tunic costume. Chain mail is not something easy to come by. I found some sequin material will give the look of chain mail if used correctly. Although it costs from sixteen to twenty dollars a yard, you will only need about a third of a yard for a costume. See Arthur Costume #2.

Arthur Costume #2

Arthur #2
Original Garment

Making the Costume

1. Dye the green dress a darker green. Cut off the bottom.
2. Cut off the bottom of the red dress. Cut out arm holes larger than they are. Glue down the edges.
3. Make large cross on front of red dress with fabric and sequins.
4. Using a wedding skull cap (see reference section), glue sequin fabric to it, leaving enough fabric to hang down neck and tuck in collar.
5. Any old shirt will work for a collar. Cover big collar with sequin fabric. Make sure you glue the edges down well on the inside of the collar.
6. Make a small neckpiece of foam covered with sequin fabric on one side. Use hook and loop tape to fasten it at the back.
7. The crown is made from a cheap felt top hat. I cut it in the shape of a crown and decorated it with sequins and fabric paint.

Arthur #2
Original Garment

8. The cape is a length of black nylon fabric that doesn't need to be hemmed. Sew or glue a hem at the top of the fabric and run a black shoestring through it to tie at the neck under the collar.

9. Shoes can be made from the bottom of the green dress. Cut two pieces for each shoe and glue them together as shown in the sketch below. Leave the bottom open.

10. Add tights and arm cuffs from the other Arthur costume. You might want to add gloves.

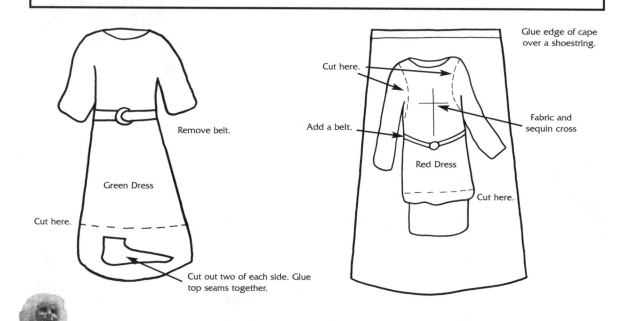

Remove belt.

Green Dress

Cut here.

Cut out two of each side. Glue top seams together.

Glue edge of cape over a shoestring.

Cut here.

Add a belt.

Red Dress

Fabric and sequin cross

Cut here.

Female and **Male Dancer** costumes are simple to create.

Making the Costume

1. Glue designs on the jumper.
2. Cut cuffs and neckline off a turtleneck shirt. Glue sequins around raw edges.
3. Make a wreath of leaves or flowers for her hair.

Female Dancer Costume

Female Dancer Original Garment

Making the Costume

1. Cut off the bottom of the dress.
2. Split the bottom of the dress in half, so you now have two rings of fabric.
3. Cut apart each ring so you have two lengths of fabric.
4. Open the seams under each arm. Then sew in the lengths of fabric from the cuffs to the hem under each arm. This will allow more space for the arms of a man.
5. Add a belt, a long-sleeved shirt, and tights.
6. The hat can be made by gluing three pieces of extra fabric together and adding a feather.

Male Dancer Costume

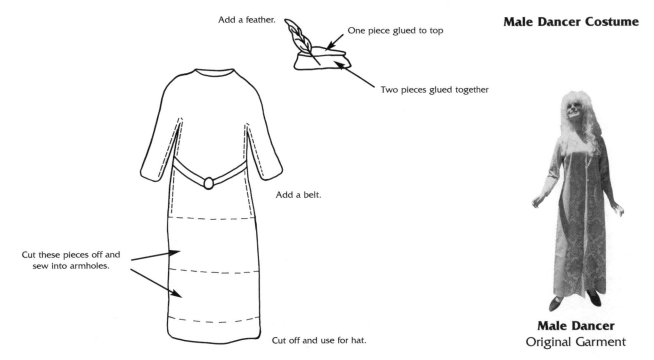

Add a feather.

One piece glued to top

Two pieces glued together

Add a belt.

Cut these pieces off and sew into armholes.

Cut off and use for hat.

Male Dancer
Original Garment

A tunic is a tunic is a tunic. Most of the men wear tunics — you may have to add or subtract accessories, but if you start with a basic tunic, anything is possible. Welcome to Camelot!

A Christmas Carol

The most commonly done production during Christmas is *A Christmas Carol*. Every year since I've been in business, I've put it together for one school or another.

The main character, of course, is **Scrooge**. I asked myself how I would make my handsome mannequin resemble a crotchety old man. Finally I decided on a mask — not exactly Scrooge, but I hope you will get the idea.

For his frock coat, I chose a man's black overcoat. It had the length I needed and would be easy to convert. See Scrooge Costume #1.

Scrooge #1

Scrooge #1
Original Garment

Making the Costume

1. Starting under the arms of the man's black overcoat, sew a piece of elastic (inside the coat) across the back and sides at the waist to give it more of a frocked look. The easiest way to do elastic is to just stretch it as you sew.
2. Glue black fake fur trim to the collar and lapels. You can make the lapels larger by extending the fake fur.
3. Glue lace inside the sleeves.
4. Use a white shirt with a large collar so it can be worn turned up, giving it a period look.
5. Add dark pants and a scarf tied into a bow at the throat.
6. Spats can be made from grey socks.
7. A large top hat — see reference section.

Scrooge #3

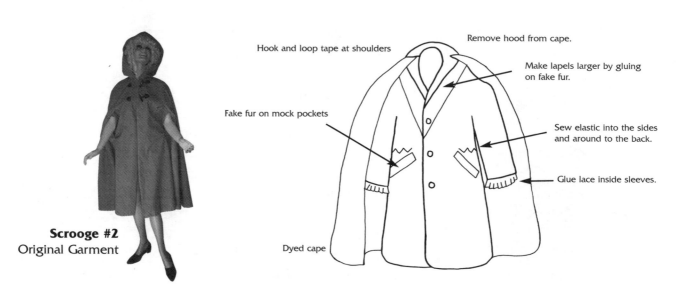

Scrooge #2

Later, Scrooge wears a cape coat. I found an old cape, cut the hood off, dyed it black, and fastened it with hook and loop tape at the shoulders, under the collar. Add a scarf and fingerless gloves for his completed outside look. See Scrooge #2.

For most of the play, Scrooge is in his night clothes. He wears a long, white, man's nightshirt, a nightcap, and a heavy robe. Well, try to find a man's long, white, nightshirt — not in my world. I searched the plus-size women's section and found several nightgowns, but none of them had the look I desired. Finally, I bought a woman's nightgown, thinking it would do — it didn't. It was great from the chest down, but the top wasn't even close. I improvised, and made the costume described in the section on *Pirates of Penzance.* It is the Major General Costume #2 on page 81. See Scrooge Costume #3.

Scrooge #2
Original Garment

Remove hood from cape.

Hook and loop tape at shoulders

Make lapels larger by gluing on fake fur.

Fake fur on mock pockets

Sew elastic into the sides and around to the back.

Glue lace inside sleeves.

Dyed cape

A lavender prom dress would be my beginning for Scrooge's one and only love, **Belle.** When the ghost took him to the past, she was a very important part of it. I wanted her in a gay party dress. The lavender prom dress would work well with a few small changes. See Belle Gown #1.

Belle Gown #1
Original Garment

Making the Costume

1. Dye lavender dress with brown and red dye.
2. Pull sheer front overlay up under the breasts and glue or fix with a brooch.
3. The dress wasn't long enough so I dyed a crinoline with blue and red dye to accent it. You could sew a large ruffle around the bottom of the skirt.
4. Add long, white gloves and a black velvet necklace.

Belle Gown #1

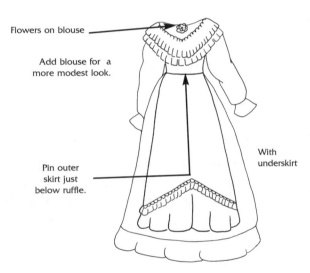

Flowers on blouse

Add blouse for a more modest look.

Pin outer skirt just below ruffle.

With underskirt

To give the same dress a more modest look, add a high-necked white blouse, with long sleeves, and a bonnet. The bonnet is made by cutting off the back half of a wide-brimmed straw hat, covering it with lace, and decorating it with ribbon and flowers. See Belle Gown #2.

For outside scenes, add a cape and a fur muff. To make a muff, cut two of the same size fake fur pieces, in the color you want, and glue them together. Pull the ends together and glue, leaving room for the hands to rest comfortably inside.

The same dress design can be used for Scrooge's niece, the women carolers, and the ladies of the town.

Belle Gown #2

For the men, see the section on *Hello, Dolly* for how to make frock coats easily and simply. They can range from poor to elegant, depending on the type of suit you use.

The ghosts can be a fun and creative process. First, you have to decide whether a woman or a man will be wearing the costume. I did the Ghost of Christmas Past as a man and the **Ghost of Christmas Present** as a woman. The Ghost of Christmas Yet-to-Come can be either because it is a concealing costume and the wearer doesn't have to speak.

In a group of dresses I bought was an old prom dress. It looked like a Christmas tree to me. It would be perfect for my Ghost of Christmas Present. See Ghost of Christmas Present Costume.

Ghost of Christmas Present

Making the Costume

1. Dye pink prom dress with two bottles of green dye.
2. Decorate the skirt much as you would decorate a Christmas tree, using green, gold, and red garland, wired garland with stars, and small decorative balls. You must concern yourself with the weight of the costume, so use lightweight, unbreakable ornaments.
3. Use a small pillbox hat, decorate it to match the dress. Add gloves.

Ghost of Christmas Present
Original Garment

You are probably wondering how in the world you could wash this dress. Turn it wrong side out, put it in a garment bag and wash it in cold water on a gentle cycle with a mild detergent. If everything is glued and tied on well, it will wash. Hang it up to dry. Christmas trim can be used outside and stands up to rain and snow, so a little washing shouldn't hurt it.

I found a great red fake fur woman's robe at a rummage sale. The arms were too small for a man, but otherwise, I knew it would work for my **Ghost of Christmas Past.** See Ghost of Christmas Past Costume.

Ghost of Christmas Past
Original Garment

Making the Costume

1. Cut the arms off the robe, cutting larger armholes to allow for the arms of a man.
2. Add a woman's full-sleeved poet-style shirt, pants, a sash belt, and boot tops. Leave the shirt open in front.
3. Cut two pieces out of the sleeves and glue them together to form the hat.
4. Trim the robe and hat with white. You can use scrap fabric from Curley's cowhide chaps in *Oklahoma!* (page 73).
5. Add silk leaves if desired.

Ghost of Christmas Past

There are no set rules on what the ghosts look like so you are free to use your imagination. I didn't do a picture of Marley's Ghost, but I will tell you an easy way to make him. Make a frock coat from an old suit. Using a box cutter, shred it. Aluminim foil, twisted and made into interlocking loops is a wonderful lightweight chain. If you want weights at the ends of the chains, make them of cardboard covered with foil. It will give you the effect you want without having to work too hard at it.

The **Ghost of Christmas Yet-to-Come** is the easiest to do. A hooded ghoul robe and a vampire cape are all you need. You may paint the actor's face or use a mask, since he is not required to speak. The ghost looks much like you might make a Grim Reaper costume. See Ghost of Christmas Yet-to-Come.

Ghost of Christmas Yet-to-Come

Tiny Tim Costume

Tiny Tim
Original Garment

Tiny Tim is a pretty simple costume. He wore a short jacket, sweater, shirt, tie, knickers, socks, scarf, and hat. I found a small woman's wool jacket I thought might work for him. See Tiny Tim Costume.

Making the Costume

1. The wool jacket was a little bit too big and the arms too long. I took in the seam down the back of the jacket and cut the arms off and glued a hem in them.
2. I cut off a pair of black, close-fitting sweatpants to make knickers.
3. I cut the sweater vest, making the length shorter, and glued a hem in.
4. Add a white shirt, tie, cap, and scarf.
5. The crutch is made by gluing a piece of foam to a stick and wrapping strips of white fabric around it.

The costumes from *A Christmas Carol* can be used in other productions from the same period, on Christmas floats, or if you are going caroling with a group.

Guys and Dolls

Gangsters in double-breasted, pinstriped suits, lady gangsters, nightclub singers in sultry gowns, and flappers are what I think of when I imagine *Guys and Dolls* on stage. Even though the original production takes place after the Roaring Twenties, every time I've been asked to costume the play, the costumes have leaned toward that time period. I will do examples ranging from the 1920s to the 1940s.

An off-white, heavy satin slip-style dress with thin straps was perfect for my first **Flapper**. It had no waist and I could use any color fringe and sequins on it. See Flapper Costume #1.

Flapper Costume #1

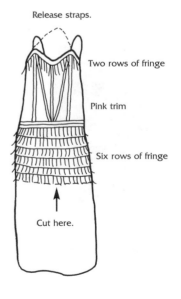

Flapper #1 Original Garment

Making the Costume

1. Cut dress to desired length.
2. Starting at hem, glue fringe and sequins in alternating shades, from light pink to red. Stop just below the waist.
3. Glue fringe and sequins around the neckline.
4. Release straps to tie behind the neck.
5. Glue pink trim on the bodice.
6. Make a headband of stretch sequins to match dress, and glue on feathers. Glue a piece of jewelry or a flower over the area in which the feathers are glued to the headband. Add a boa. (See reference section.)

Release straps.

Two rows of fringe

Pink trim

Six rows of fringe

Cut here.

Flapper Costume #2

A black sequined prom dress with a white flounce was purchased for another flapper. Some women don't like the bareness of the thin-strapped dress used for Flapper #1, so this is another option. See Flapper Costume #2.

Making the Costume

1. Release the white skirt from the bottom of the dress. Put it aside for later use in this chapter.
2. Remove the bow and white flower.
3. Glue long fringe around the bottom of the dress. Glue sequin trim over that.
4. Glue flower and bow to black hat.
5. Add long beads and a feather boa.

Flapper #2
Original Garment

Remove flower and glue to hat.

Remove skirt.
Add fringe and sequins.

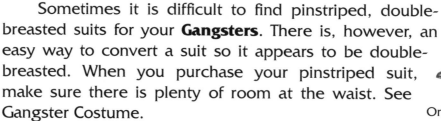

Gangster Costume

Gangster
Original Garment

Sometimes it is difficult to find pinstriped, double-breasted suits for your **Gangsters**. There is, however, an easy way to convert a suit so it appears to be double-breasted. When you purchase your pinstriped suit, make sure there is plenty of room at the waist. See Gangster Costume.

Making the Costume

1. Move buttons over a few inches.
2. Glue on extra buttons next to them.
3. Add a white shirt, red tie, and hat.
4. Spats can be made by cutting socks to cover the top of the shoes and tacking two pieces of thin elastic in front of the heel.
5. For this production, you will want suspenders under the suits for that period look.

For our **Lady Gangster**, I found a really tacky, three-piece, pinstriped suit at a rummage sale. All I did was shorten the skirt and hem it, add a blouse, a tie, a piece of velvet and a handkerchief for the mock pocket, and a beret. See Lady Gangster Costume.

Lady Gangster Costume

Red silk handkerchief

Add a piece of velvet.

Hem skirt.

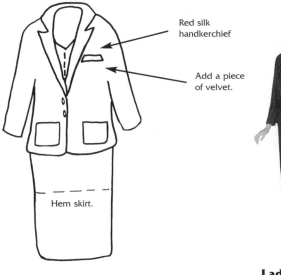

Lady Gangster
Original Garment

Twenties Gown

With three **Sultry Gowns**, I'll show you the range of periods you can use for the production of *Guys and Dolls*.

Making the Costume

1. Dye the white, sleeved dress red.
2. Dye the white slip dress pink.
3. Remove sleeves and collar from the neck of the now red dress.
4. Remove the lace from the bodice.
5. Glue sequin trim around armholes, neck, and diagonally across one side of bodice.
6. The pink boa is attached with hook and loop tape so it can be removed for washing.
7. Put the red dress over the pink slip.
8. The hat was the dome of a straw hat, with sequins glued on and a feather and flower added for decoration. Add long gloves and a choker. (See reference section.)

Twenties Gown
Original Garment

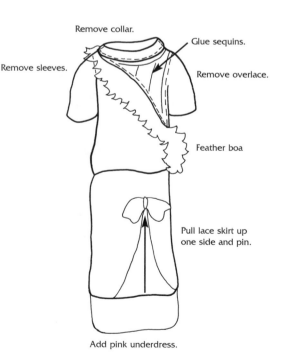

Remove collar.

Glue sequins.

Remove sleeves.

Remove overlace.

Feather boa

Pull lace skirt up one side and pin.

Add pink underdress.

Twenties Gown
Original Garment

Making the Costume

1. Remove the white flounce and bow from the black sequinned dress.
2. Remove the black underskirting from the flowered dress.
3. Glue the black underskirting to the sequinned dress.
4. Glue a line of wide black sequins where you attached the two fabrics. It will cover the area and help it stay on better.
5. Add a line of rhinestones down the front of the gown. Glue bow to the back.
6. Add a boa and long white gloves.

Tip: This dress could also be used for the production of *Gypsy.*

Mid-Thirties Gown

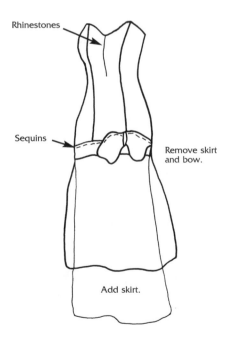

Rhinestones

Sequins

Remove skirt and bow.

Add skirt.

Mid-Thirties Gown
Original Garment

Mid-Thirties Gown
Original Garment

Mid-Thirties Gown
Original Garment

Late Thirties Gown

Making the Costume

1. Dye lavender dress with one bottle of black dye, running it through only one cycle to get the silver grey color.
2. Carefully remove the sleeves, the sash, and all lace from the dress.
3. Sew the lace around the hem of the dress to make it a long dress. It will only go halfway around.
4. Bring the edges of the lace together and pin them up on the side.
5. Glue sash and bow to cover the pins.
6. Glue fringe to a shawl and add long black gloves.

Late Thirties Gown
Original Garment

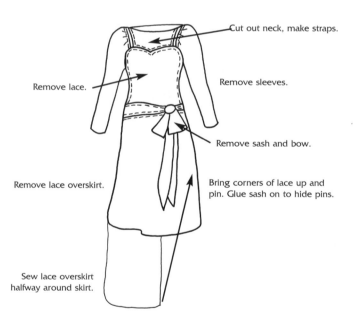

Cut out neck, make straps.

Remove lace.

Remove sleeves.

Remove sash and bow.

Remove lace overskirt.

Bring corners of lace up and pin. Glue sash on to hide pins.

Sew lace overskirt halfway around skirt.

Calypso Costume

When I made Flapper Costume #2, I told you we would save the white flounce for later use. When the production takes us to Havana, you will need a sexy **Calypso** style dress. By combining an old fringed dress with the white flounce, I believe I have achieved the look. See Calypso Costume.

Making the Costume

1. Cut the bottom of the dress off at an angle, front and back.
2. Glue the large white flounce to the angled hem of the dress.
3. Glue the trim above the flounce, overlapping enough to hide the seam.
4. Use excess trim to decorate the neckline and back of the dress.
5. Add a fringed shawl, hat, and corset.

Tip: The corset may be made by covering two pieces of cardboard with lace, attaching them together with spandex in the back, and with shoe-strings in front.

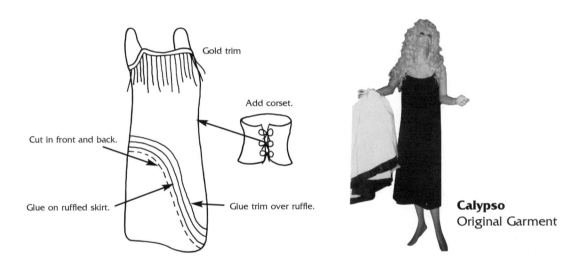

Gold trim

Add corset.

Cut in front and back.

Glue on ruffled skirt.

Glue trim over ruffle.

Calypso
Original Garment

Guys and Dolls can have a broad range of costumes from the twenties to the early forties. I'm sure the reason a lot of people lean toward the twenties costumes is because they are a little more flamboyant and glitzy and look better on stage.

For streetwear, see the section on *Annie*. Many of those costumes can be used for this production. To make a "mission" costume for a woman, see the section on Grace #1 (page 14). Grace's tailored suit could have been dyed navy blue, with a bonnet and white gloves added. For the man's "mission" costume, see the East Indian Manservant (page 17). Again, with navy blue dye, a white shirt and tie, and a different hat — it would work.

Although there are a lot of men's costumes in *Guys and Dolls*, they are all basically the same, though with different colors.

Hello, Dolly

My favorite production is *Hello, Dolly*. I was fortunate enough to see it at the Municipal Opera in St. Louis many years ago and have never forgotten it. I loved the glitz and glamour of the costumes.

Some time ago, I was given an old red prom dress. It didn't look like much so I washed it, put it on a hanger and forgot about it. When it was time to make **Dolly**'s famous red and black dress, I remembered I had it put away. See Dolly #1.

Dolly #1

Dolly #1
Original Garment

Making the Costume

1. Remove flounce around the bodice top, sleeves, and roses from the skirt.
2. Remove the underskirting.
3. Release gathers in the overskirt and press the wrinkles out.
4. Cut two Vs out of black skirt, leaving the top of one V attached to the elastic waist.
5. Attach the second V to the neckline of bodice, with the point down.
6. Glue the second V directly to the bodice.
7. Cut the elastic waist of the first V in the middle of the back and add hook and loop tape to hold it on.
8. Glue black fringe around the edges of the Vs and glue alternate red, gold, and black sequins to cover.

Dolly #1
Original Garment

9. At the neckline, cover where you glued with stretch black sequins, bringing them over the shoulders for straps. Glue a piece of fringe and sequins around each shoulder.
10. The headpiece is a wide headband with feathers and sequins glued on. Add boa and long gloves.

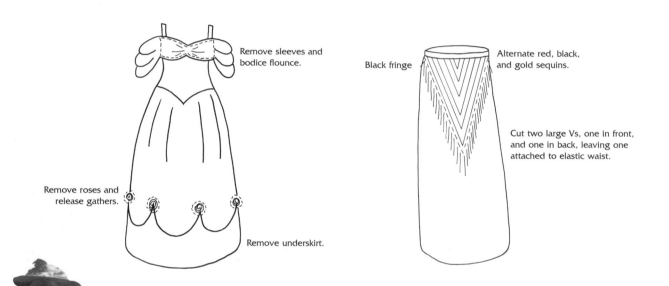

Remove sleeves and bodice flounce.

Remove roses and release gathers.

Remove underskirt.

Black fringe

Alternate red, black, and gold sequins.

Cut two large Vs, one in front, and one in back, leaving one attached to elastic waist.

Among a group of couples, Dolly sang and danced to a number called, "Put On Your Sunday Clothes." Her costume was an orange and red two-piece dress with a small cape and a large hat. See Dolly #2.

Dolly #2

Making the Costume

1. Dye plaid skirt and blouse with tangerine dye.
2. Pin and glue orange ribbon to both sides of red cummerbund to tie in back.

Dolly #2
Original Garment

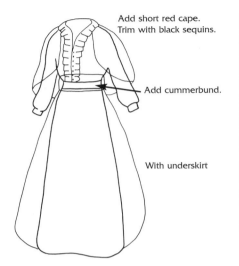

Add short red cape.
Trim with black sequins.

Add cummerbund.

With underskirt

3. Use a red skirt to make cape. Attach at shoulders with hook and loop tape. Trim with black sequins.
4. Add a white blouse with ruffles at the neck and wrist. Attach an orange flower at the throat.
5. Add a crinoline for fullness.
6. Use an old straw hat, painted orange and decorated with feathers, flowers, and a bow. Add white gloves.

The **Couples** on stage with Dolly for "Put On Your Sunday Clothes" are matched. If the woman has a pink dress, the man has a pink suit. It is so cleverly done. I have included two couples as examples of the supporting costumes you might need. I've done a silver grey couple and a pink and red couple. The silver grey couple's costumes are fancier. See Man's Frock Coat Costume and Lady in Grey Costume.

Man's Frock Coat Costume

Man's Frock Coat
Original Garment

Making the Costume

1. Cut the legs off the suit pants at the crotch.
2. Cut out the inseams. Press the creases out of the pants.
3. Place fabric so cuffs are up. Glue the two pieces together at one corner.
4. Glue down cut edges.
5. Beginning in the center of the back of the coat, glue around to the front, just under the button at the waist.

6. Add darker pants, vest, white shirt, and ascot tie. A top hat is a must for this costume. (See reference section.)

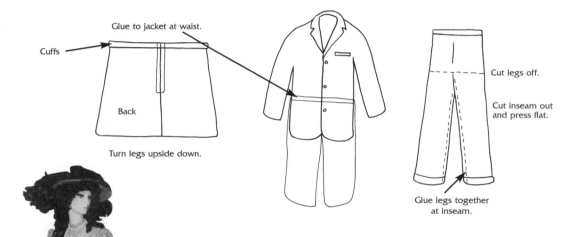

Cuffs

Glue to jacket at waist.

Back

Turn legs upside down.

Cut legs off.

Cut inseam out and press flat.

Glue legs together at inseam.

Lady in Grey Costume

Making the Costume

1. Dye wedding dress with black dye through one washer cycle.
2. Using black fabric paint, I made small buttons down the center front of the sheer bodice and added a row around the edge of the lace where the fabric meets the sheer.
3. Spray paint a straw hat silver and glue on feathers.
4. Add beads and gloves.

Tip: If you would like authentic looking shoes, you could use a pair of grey socks and black stretchy house slippers. With your fabric paint, make buttons on the front or side of the socks.

Lady in Grey
Original Garment

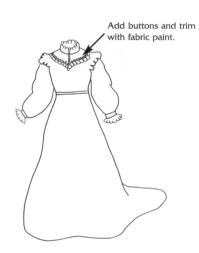

Add buttons and trim with fabric paint.

The second couple, pink and red, although very nice, are not as fancy as the first. In this scene, there is a large range of colorful couples wearing their Sunday best. See Pink Man and Pink Lady.

Pink Man
Original Garment

Making the Costume

1. Dye a light-colored suit with red dye through one washer cycle to get the pink look.
2. Remove the existing buttons from the jacket.
3. Using four matching buttons, sew the top one up farther, and glue the others on below. Add a piece of hook and loop tape high up to hold the jacket closed.
4. Add shirt, red tie, spats made from socks, and a straw boater hat. (See reference section.)

Pink Man Costume

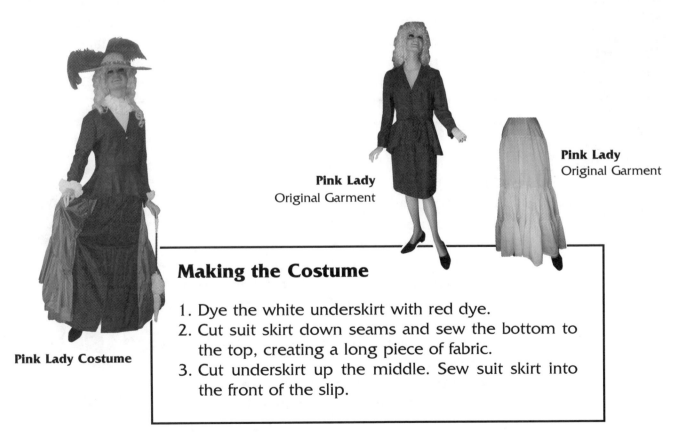

Pink Lady
Original Garment

Pink Lady
Original Garment

Pink Lady Costume

Making the Costume

1. Dye the white underskirt with red dye.
2. Cut suit skirt down seams and sew the bottom to the top, creating a long piece of fabric.
3. Cut underskirt up the middle. Sew suit skirt into the front of the slip.

4. Add white blouse with ruffles at neck and wrist and a parasol.
5. The large straw hat has the brim glued up in the back and feathers, sequins, and flowers glued on.

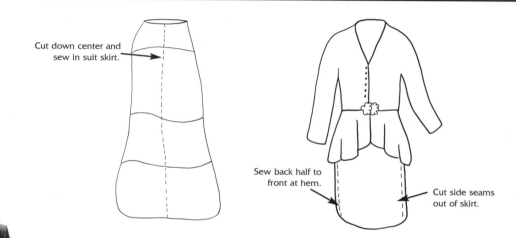

Cut down center and sew in suit skirt.

Sew back half to front at hem.

Cut side seams out of skirt.

Horace Vandergelder is singing about "gettin' to the church on time" for his marriage to Dolly. Period suits aren't easy to come by, but I've discovered an easy way to make them. You will need to buy a jacket and pants that match well. See Cutaway Period Suit.

Cutaway Period Suit

Making the Costume

1. Cut the legs off the suit pants at the crotch.
2. Cut along inseam of both legs. Lay out flat and press the creases out.
3. Glue two pieces together at one corner.
4. Glue down the cut edges.
5. Glue the legs to the jacket, beginning at the center of the back, coming around to the front just under the button at the waist. Glue front flaps and jacket front back.
6. Add lighter colored pants, a vest, white shirt, and ascot tie.
7. Add a flower on the left breast pocket of jacket.
8. Add spats made from socks and a short top hat.

Cutaway Period Suit
Original Garment

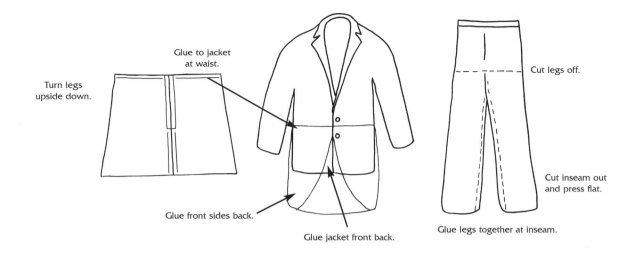

Turn legs upside down.

Glue to jacket at waist.

Glue front sides back.

Glue jacket front back.

Cut legs off.

Cut inseam out and press flat.

Glue legs together at inseam.

Dolly #3
Original Garment

Dolly is waiting at the church all dressed in white. She has a long dress with large puffed sleeves and a big hat with white flowers and feathers. I used the outer skirt from the wedding dress that made the Guenevere Costume #2 in the *Camelot* section (page 31). See Dolly #3.

Dolly #3
Original Garment

Dolly #3 Costume

Making the Costume

1. Cut the skirting off the short white dress.
2. Turn sheer white nightie backwards to tie at neck in back. Sheer white nightie to be worn on top of lacy short dress. Puff the sleeves up above the longer lace sleeves of the short dress.
3. Glue the edges of the waist down on the wedding dress outer skirt and attach hook and loop tape to the back.

4. Add a crinoline for fullness and a sash belt that is long enough to tie into a bow in the back.
5. Add a brooch at neck and white gloves.
6. The hat is a large, brimmed straw hat, spray painted white, with feathers, netting, and flowers glued on.

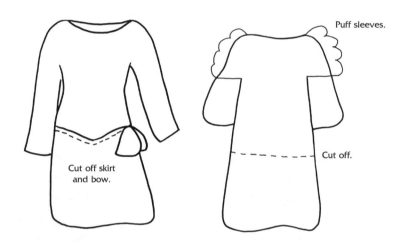

Puff sleeves.

Cut off skirt
and bow.

Cut off.

I hope I have given you enough examples for a wonderful production of *Hello, Dolly*. You can get many different costumes by purchasing light colored suits and dyeing them different colors. Different hats make them look more individual. Try to keep your colors similar for couples.

The King and I

Anna arrives in Siam on a ship, wearing a traveling suit. It can be any color you wish. When I did the chapter on *Hello, Dolly* I told you I would be using the costume from the Pink Lady later. When I decided to do Anna's traveling suit, I realized that by turning the skirt backwards and adding different accessories and a hoop skirt — the outfit was done. I couldn't believe it. See what you think. See Anna Costume #1.

Anna Costume #1

**Pink Lady
Costume**

Making the Costume

See directions for Pink Lady
  Costume on page 55.
1. Turn skirt around so that the brocade strip goes down the back.
2. Add a full hoop skirt.
3. Glue lace around the neck of a white blouse and add a matching colored ribbon.
4. Put jacket over the blouse.
5. Hat is made of a piece of foam cut in an oval and covered with lines of ruffled lace and a ribbon to hold it on.

Pink Lady
Original Garment

Pink lady
Original Garment

I was given an old prom dress that had certainly seen better days. I tried to take the color out, to no avail; however, it did lighten the dress. I decided finally to try dyeing it with gold dye to see how the color would come out. It made the dress an almost copper color. I liked it. This dress would work for Anna's ballgown. See Anna Costume #2.

Anna #2 Costume

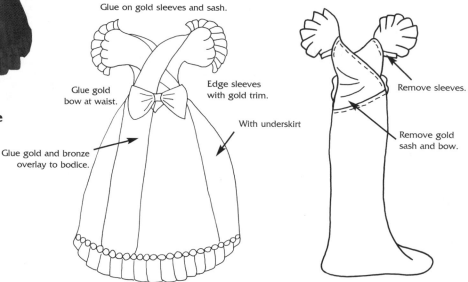

Glue on gold sleeves and sash.

Glue gold bow at waist.

Edge sleeves with gold trim.

With underskirt

Glue gold and bronze overlay to bodice.

Remove sleeves.

Remove gold sash and bow.

Anna #2
Original Garment

Anna #2
Original Garment

Making the Costume

1. Dye red dress with gold dye.
2. Cut gold sash, sleeves, and bow off gold and black dress.
3. Fix the gold sleeves directly over the existing sleeves, gluing them down and gluing the sash to the front of the bodice at an angle.
4. Cut bronze and gold overlay off dress that will be used for the Siamese wife. (See page 63.)
5. Cut seam out of overlay. Taking one corner, glue it to the bodice on the opposite side from the gold. Glue it down to the waist, crossing over the gold sash.
6. Glue gold trim to all raw edges at bodice and sleeves.
7. Glue down raw edges of overlay and large bow at center of waist.
8. Add a stiff underskirt and long gloves.

I have made the **King of Siam** costume many times, from elaborate to very plain. He can be what you want him to be depending on how much work you are willing to put in. Some just use blousy pants, while others want the more traditional Siamese look. I have done him both ways so you can decide for yourself what type of look you desire.

I have always used graduation gowns for his shirts. They work better than anything else I could find and they dye well. See King of Siam Costume #1.

**King of Siam
Costume #1**

King of Siam #1
Original Garment

Making the Costume

1. Dye white graduation gown with red dye.
2. Remove zipper. Glue edges down.
3. Cut off and hem at desired length.
4. Trim with gold at neck and sleeves.
5. Cut gold pants off at an angle and hem.

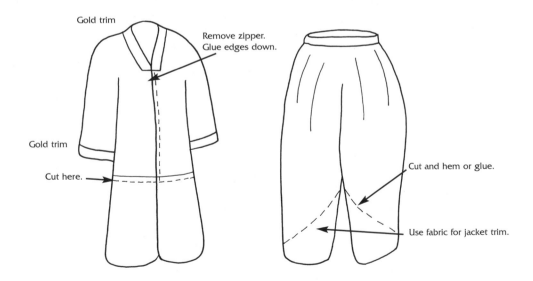

Gold trim

Remove zipper.
Glue edges down.

Gold trim

Cut here.

Cut and hem or glue.

Use fabric for jacket trim.

If you want a much fancier King of Siam with the Siamese pants, I'll show you how. See King of Siam Costume #2.

King of Siam Costume #2

King of Siam #2
Original Garment

Making the Costume

1. Cut black graduation gown at desired length, making it longer in the back. Remove zipper.
2. Trim with gold sequins and circles of gold lame fabric. When you glue the fabric circles on, either go around them with fabric paint or glue on lined sequins to keep them from fraying.
3. Cut the inseam out of the black pants. Sew up like a skirt.
4. Cut and hem pants (now skirt) so they are much longer in the front.
5. Pull longer front up between legs and fasten to back of waist with pins. Glue sequin trim on legs and run up the back to cover pins. You should glue black fabric over pins on the inside of the waist to avoid pins coming loose.
6. Cut circles out of same fabric used for the top and glue them on, edging them with either fabric paint or lined sequins.

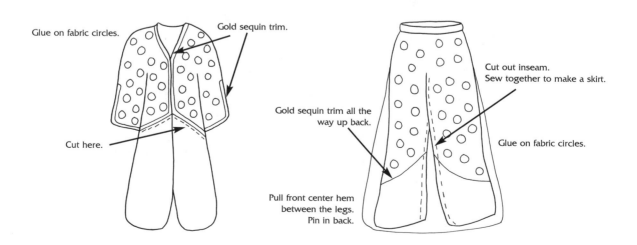

Glue on fabric circles.

Gold sequin trim.

Cut here.

Cut out inseam.
Sew together to make a skirt.

Gold sequin trim all the way up back.

Glue on fabric circles.

Pull front center hem between the legs. Pin in back.

The king has many **Siamese wives**. I've done one wife to show you how. You can make many different ones by using the same idea but different dresses and colors. See Siamese Wife Costume.

Siamese Wife
Original Garment

Siamese Wife
Original Garment

Siamese Wife Costume

Making the Costume

1. Remove the ruffle from the gold dress. Cut into pieces for chest ruffle and cuffs.
2. Cut around the waist, leaving a long flap of fabric in the front.
3. Glue the gold ruffle across one side of the dress bodice.
4. Glue gold trim and turquoise trim over the gold ruffle at bodice, extending it around the waist, but not over the flap.
5. Trim the gold flap with gold trim.
6. Using scraps from the gold dress, make a ruffle and glue on cuffs. Glue gold and turquoise trim over that. Add gold trim at neck.
7. You have already removed the gold and bronze overlay from the other dress to use on Anna's ballgown. The underskirt is brown satin.
8. For the Siamese pants look, tack a piece of thin elastic to the center of the front hem and run it through the legs to the bottom of the zipper in back. Tack it there. It will give you the look you want and your actress can move easily in it. If you want it to be a dress, merely leave the elastic out of it.

9. The hat is a piece of foam, covered with scraps from the gold dress, glued together to form a circle. Add decoration to match the dress.

Tip: When making the hat, put a loop of elastic at each side so you can use two bobby pins to hold it on.

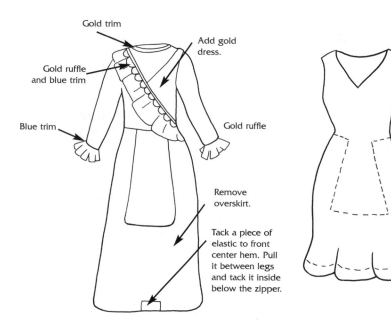

Gold trim

Add gold dress.

Gold ruffle and blue trim

Blue trim

Gold ruffle

Remove overskirt.

Tack a piece of elastic to front center hem. Pull it between legs and tack it inside below the zipper.

Cut here.

Cut and divide for chest ruffle and cuffs.

Mame

Mame loves unusual, attention-getting costumes, so you can have a great deal of fun and be very creative with her.

The play takes place in New York and begins in 1928, ending in 1946. I've chosen four costumes as examples of the range you will be working with.

If the first gown looks familiar, it's because I made it for *Guys and Dolls* and changed the accessories. By adding long gloves and a large feathered hat, I've given it that Mame look. See Mame #1.

In one scene, Mame has to wear a riding costume. She can't ride a horse, but she looks the part. I call this type of costume a "throw together" because it is just a matter of putting the right pieces together, with no sewing. See Mame #2.

Mame #1

Mame #2

Making the Costume

1. The skirt was left over from the black and gold dress used in *The King and I* section (page 60). Make sure the zipper is all the way down when you cut a skirt off a dress. Merely glue the edge of the waist down, including the top of the zipper on both sides. You will be amazed how quickly you can have a skirt.

2. Add a white, high-necked blouse, a black tie and jacket, white gloves, and a short top hat with a feather.

Cut skirt off. Glue edges down.

Mame #3

In a later scene, Mame wears a Russian costume. When I found a vest dress at a thrift shop, that was the costume I saw. The costume is a high-necked black blouse, a black skirt, that wonderful long vest, and a hat. The hat was made by gluing two pieces of lamb's wool together, spraying them grey and adding some black fabric paint to make the hat match the vest. See Mame #3.

I always remember Mame at the top of a spiral staircase, making her entrance in a stunning black gown. I didn't have a black gown I thought would work well, but I located a shiny, black pantsuit that could do the job. See Mame #4.

If you need men's tuxedos for the production, check with your local rental shop to see if they have used tuxes they wish to sell. If you are unable to do that, look in the reference section to see where to buy them wholesale.

Mame #3
Original
Garment

Mame #4

Mame #4
Original Garment

Making the Costume

1. Remove the collar and belt, snipping off any belt loops.
2. Cut the inseam out of the pants. This is a very stretchy fabric so it will give well.
3. Sew inseams together to make a skirt, leaving a split in one side.
4. Glue black fringe around hem of top, hem of skirt, up the slit, and into the cuffs.
5. With hook and loop tape, fasten a boa over one arm, up to the shoulder and across the back.

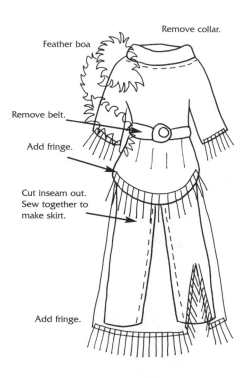

Feather boa

Remove collar.

Remove belt.

Add fringe.

Cut inseam out. Sew together to make skirt.

Add fringe.

My Fair Lady

My Fair Lady begins outside Covent Gardens in London, 1912. **Eliza Doolittle** is dressed in an old straw hat, old clothing, and an apron and shawl. She wears shoddy clothing throughout the early scenes. You should be able to manage these costumes as "throw togethers."

The most famous gown in My Fair Lady is the black and white gown worn for the Ascot scene. It looks much more difficult than it is. See Eliza Ascot Gown.

Eliza Ascot Gown

Eliza Ascot Gown
Original Garment

Making the Costume

1. The long-sleeved dress is a two-piece. The underdress is like a slip and the overdress is white lace with sleeves. Separate the two because you will be working with glue and you don't want it to go through. The other dress will be used for the black and white fabric. Save the upper portion of the dress because we will use it in another costume in this chapter.
2. I found a dress (not pictured) with a white lace flounce. Remove the flounce and sew it onto the bottom of the slip-like underdress.
3. Cut the hem off the black and white dress and glue it to the hem of the white lace overdress.
4. Remove the black and white sash and cut it in half. Glue half of it around the chest and half around the hip of the lace overlay dress.
5. Cut strips from black and white skirt, glue down edges and make bows. Glue them to the chest, hip, hem, and a parasol.

Eliza Ascot Gown
Original Garment

6. Glue white ruffled lace at the neck and cuffs. Glue a piece of black ribbon on the cuffs just above the lace.

7. A large-brimmed straw hat was spray-painted white, a bow, feathers, and flowers added, and a mop hat glued inside one side finished off the costume. (For instructions on how to make a mop hat, see page 102.) Add white gloves for a more elegant look.

Remove sash.

Cut four strips.

Remove bottom of dress.

Cut sash in half and glue to bust and hip.

Glue ruffled lace to neck.

Make bows from skirt and glue on.

Lace ruffles at wrists
Black ribbon above ruffle

Glue striped fabric from hem on lace overdress.

Sew flounce to underdress.

Black and White Supporting Dress

Everyone always hates to do the Ascot scene because of all the **Supporting Characters** in black and white costumes, but they do not have to be difficult if you use a layered look. When you do that, you can make the gowns very quickly. I've made one as an example of what the other women in the scene might wear. See Black and White Supporting Dress.

Black and White Supporting Dress
Original Garment

Making the Costume

1. Glue an edge of lace at the cuffs and bodice of the long black dress.
2. Hem the remainder of the black and white striped dress (see page 67) and pull the center of the hem to the waist from underneath. Pin it.
3. Remove the straps of the striped dress and glue the points of the bodice and the waist to the black dress.
4. Make a hat the same way I did for Eliza's Ascot gown.

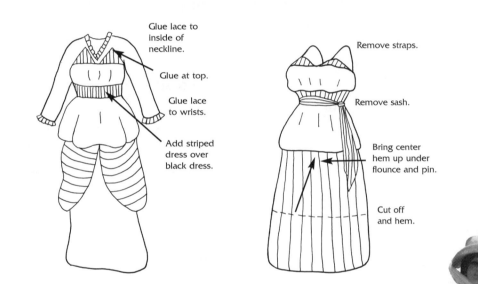

Glue lace to inside of neckline.

Glue at top.

Glue lace to wrists.

Add striped dress over black dress.

Remove straps.

Remove sash.

Bring center hem up under flounce and pin.

Cut off and hem.

You should be able to make any number of quick and easy, but still appropriate, gowns for the Ascot scene, using the layered method.

For the men's costumes, see the *Hello, Dolly* section on how to make cutaway coats and frock coats.

Eliza's leaving and she's wearing an orange, baggy suit of the period. Well, I couldn't find anything in a suit that would resemble her costume. I ended up buying a long jacket and long skirt that could be easily converted into a traveling suit. See Eliza Costume #2.

Eliza Costume #2

Eliza #2
Original Garment

Making the Costume

1. Dye skirt and jacket with tangerine dye, letting it agitate through three cycles.
2. Turn the skirt inside out and sew down both sides, leaving it fuller from the hip to the thigh and tighter at the bottom. Cut away excess fabric.
3. Move the button up on the jacket to give it the look you desire.
4. Using fabric clipped off the inside of the skirt, make two triangles by gluing two pieces together. Glue them to the front of the jacket, just below the shoulders.
5. I glued some trim from an old bridal veil to the end of the triangles for decoration.
6. The hat is a short, brimmed straw hat, with flowers and netting glued on.
7. Glue white lace around the collar of a white blouse and add white gloves and short boot shoes to complete the look.

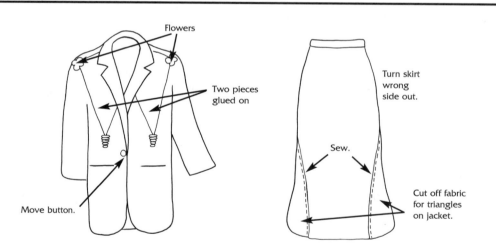

Eliza #3

Like Cinderella, Eliza got to attend the ball. The search was on for the perfect dress to convert into her ballgown. I bought a white prom dress and a sheer white nightgown. When combined, these would make a beautiful, elegant gown. See Eliza #3.

Eliza #3
Original Garment

Eliza #3
Original Garment

Making the Costume

1. Remove the ruffle from the bodice and the lace overskirt from the white prom dress.
2. Cut the sheer nightie off under the arms, all the way around.
3. Lay the nightie fabric out on a flat surface and decorate with drops of fabric paint. Let dry.
4. Drape the nightie around the back of the prom dress and pin corners together just under the bust in the center. Glue and cover with a brooch.
5. Following the lace design of the bodice, use gold, white pearl, silver, and black pearl fabric paint to give it a beaded look.
6. Cut off the cuffs of the nightie. Glue them together and attach a small ribbon in back to tie around the neck. Repeat the same fabric paint design you used on the bodice. Glue tiny beads to the neckpiece.
7. The tiara is made of pipe cleaners glued together and drops of fabric paint. Add long white gloves.

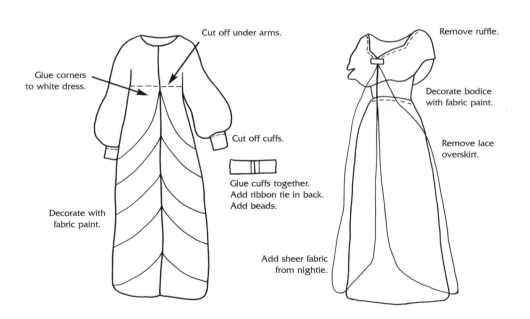

Higgins Costume

The same white dress and sheer nightie I used for this costume were used to make the wedding dress for the section on *Oklahoma*, before I cut it up.

The men's costumes used in this production can be found in other sections, such as, *Hello, Dolly*, where I show you how to make cutaway coats and frock coats. Used tuxedos can be purchased through rental shops or from a wholesale company listed in the reference section of this book.

I put together the tweed suit **Professor Higgins** wore in the production. It was a matter of finding the right pieces. See Higgins Costume.

Oklahoma!

Western wear has been relatively easy for me to find because I live in Arizona. The thrift shops and rummage sales abound with shirts, pants, cowboy hats and boots. However, when I realized I would need a pair of cowhide chaps for **Curley**, the quest began. Where in the world would I find cowhide, and if I did, what would I do with it? As a vegetarian and an animal lover, the thought wasn't pretty. Now, I had the question of how to make them out of synthetic fabric that would be convincing.

I scoured the fabric shops and finally found a sale table that held a synthetic fabric that resembled a thinner version of lamb's wool. They had it in black and white. I bought two yards of white and a half-yard of black.

Curley #1

For Curley, I put together a white western shirt with dark piping, dark striped pants, a belt, and a dark cowboy hat. See Curley #1.

By adding chaps to the existing costume, Curley took on a different look. See Curley #2.

Curley #2

Making the Costume

1. Lay the white fabric out on the floor. Lay Curley's pants flat on the fabric and cut around them leaving several inches extra around the legs.
2. Glue or sew a seam at the waist and attach a hook and loop tape fastener to the back. It will be covered by his belt so no one will see it.
3. Glue odd-cut shapes of black fabric on the white for a cow-like look.
4. Cut out the center of the top of the chaps where the pants should show through.
5. With excess black fabric, cut two pieces and glue them on the back of the chaps, leaving plenty of room for the legs to go through.
6. Put belt over the top of the chaps.

Country Dress
Original Garment

Ado Annie

Cowboy #1

Country Dress

Cowboy #2

Bad Guy Cowboy Jud

If you cannot find toy guns at toy stores or rummage sales, see the reference section of this book for places to buy toy guns wholesale.

By adding a ruffled apron to a prom dress, you can come up with the dresses for the **Country Women** for this production. Are you familiar with those eating establishments, popping up all over the country, that have country gift shops in the lobby? I found an apron there for twelve dollars. Since the prom gown was given to me, I didn't feel that was too much to pay. If your dress is dark-colored, leave the apron white, and if the dress is light-colored, you can dye the apron whatever color you like. You will need a crinoline under the dress. See Country Dress.

Ado Annie tends to dress a little more provocatively then the rest of the women. I already had a dress that would work for her. See the section on *Annie Get Your Gun*. It is the dress used for the Town Woman.

For the other **Cowboys**, I've put together two examples. The first, cowboy daywear, is a cowboy shirt with a design on it, tan pants, a belt, a hat, and boots. All parts of this costume were purchased at rummage sales. See Cowboy #1.

If you need a dressier cowboy costume, buy a western-cut jacket and add fringe. Put it together with a vest, shirt, string tie, pants, and hat. If you can't find string ties, see the reference section. See Cowboy #2.

There always has to be a cowboy bad guy. **Jud** is the bad guy in *Oklahoma!* I think bad guys always wear pinstriped pants — at least, mine do. I found a western-cut jacket, put it together with the pants, a black vest, tie, hat, and a white shirt. I think he looks mean enough. See Bad Guy Cowboy Jud.

Laurey and Curley are getting married. I needed a period wedding dress for the bride. I found a white, lacy prom dress but it needed a higher neck and long sleeves. A white sheer nightie saved the day. See Laurey Wedding Gown.

Making the Costume

1. Cut the nightie off just below the waist. It doesn't need hemming because it won't fray.
2. Put the ruffled prom dress over the nightie and add a crinoline.
3. Add a wedding veil.

Laurey Wedding Gown

**Laurey
Wedding Gown**
Original Garment

**Laurey
Wedding Gown**
Original Garment

The white prom dress and sheer nightie were used earlier to make the ballgown for Eliza Doolittle in the section on *My Fair Lady.*

If you use pretty party dresses with the aprons, you can remove the apron, add hats and accessories, and have completely different costumes for the women.

Pirates of Penzance

The **Major General** is an important character. In the early part of the play, he is dressed in military style with a long red coat. Again, I have opted for the use of a lab coat. You can use some creative judgment when doing the Major General as long as the basic idea comes across to the audience. I've dressed him several different ways. See Major General #1.

Major General #1

Major General #1
Original Garment

Making the Costume

1. Dye the lab coat red.
2. Glue lower front coat corners back to give it a cutaway look.
3. Make epaulettes for the shoulders and glue them on. They can be made of foam, covered with gold fabric, and edged with fringe.
4. The medals can be made with striped fabric and fabric paint. Glue them directly to front of jacket.
5. Glue gold trim around sleeves near the cuffs.
6. Add a white shirt, tight-fitting pants, a belt, a sash, and a tie.
7. Boot tops are easy to make from leather-like fabrics. See the sketch on page 22. If you don't wish to make them, they can be bought through several wholesale companies. See reference section.
8. I used a pith helmet for the Major General. You can also use a cocked hat with a plume.

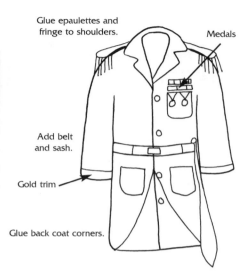

Glue epaulettes and fringe to shoulders.

Medals

Add belt and sash.

Gold trim

Glue back coat corners.

9. A possible prop for the Major General is an umbrella. I glued ball fringe on an old umbrella for the desired effect.
10. See the reference section to purchase a monocle.

The **Pirate King** is flashy and fierce. One of the essentials for any pirate is a full-sleeved shirt. These are difficult to find in the men's department. If you look in the plus-sized women's clothing sections, you will be much more likely to find a blouse with large puffed sleeves and ruffles at the cuffs. Sometimes I buy large women's nightgowns with the right kind of sleeves and hem them.

Do you really need a coat or will a long, flashy vest work as well? They are easier to make and more comfortable for the actor. If you insist on a coat, buy old dressing gowns and convert them. For the purpose of this book, I will use the long vest look. See Pirate King Costume.

Pirate King Costume

Making the Costume

1. Cut the sleeves and bottom off the red satin robe and hem both.
2. Cut the woman's black velvet dress, with elastic waist, up the front. Cut sleeves off, leaving small cap sleeves at shoulders.
3. Glue gold trim on edges, including capped sleeves.
4. Place the black, long vest over the puffy-sleeved shirt. Place the red long vest over that for a layered pirate look.

Pirate King
Original Garment

Pirate King
Original Garment

> 5. Add a pair of tight-fitting pants, tall boot tops, and a pirate hat with feather garnish.
> 6. Cut a "U" out of fabric. Glue a piece of ribbon to the top to tie behind the neck. Glue layers of ruffled trim on it. That will be your neck ruffle.
> 7. I couldn't find the kind of belt I wanted so I made a red sash out of fabric I had left from Dolly's dress (page 51) and made a mock belt of black fabric and fabric paint. Tie at the side of waist.

Frederick is the apprentice to the Pirate King. He will wear a pirate suit, but not as fancy as the Pirate King. If you remove the red vest, add a plainer hat and shorter boots, you will have a costume to suit him. See Frederick Costume.

Again, if you wish to have jackets, you can use dressing gowns. See Captain Hook's Costume from the section on *Peter Pan*. It is the same idea, but using a top coat.

See the reference section to purchase wholesale swords and wigs for pirates.

The rest of the men wear all types of more common pirate costumes. You should be able to find everything you need in the thrift shops, except maybe the hats and swords.

TIP: It's easier to sew a hoop on a scarf that will be worn over one ear than to try to get everyone to find an earring that will work. Plus, they won't fall off.

Frederick Costume

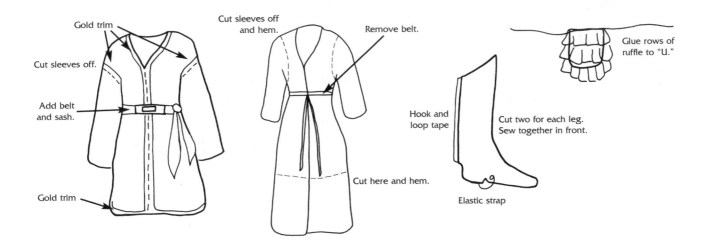

Gold trim

Cut sleeves off.

Add belt and sash.

Gold trim

Cut sleeves off and hem.

Remove belt.

Cut here and hem.

Hook and loop tape

Cut two for each leg. Sew together in front.

Elastic strap

Glue rows of ruffle to "U."

Ruth, the Pirate Wench, is a plump, middle-aged woman. I couldn't make my mannequin look older or fatter, but I've tried to give you an idea of the costume. Use your imagination. See Pirate Wench Costume.

Cut here.
Glue edge under.

Pirate Wench Costume

Making the Costume

1. Dye the drawstring top blue. It already has boning in the front, under the breasts, so you can cut off the top part and glue down the edge.
2. Pin one side of a colorful skirt up to show underskirting.
3. Dye underskirt red.
4. Add white, blousy, sleeved shirt, vest, boot tops, and hat.

Mabel is the Major General's daughter. She will need a pretty dress with a tight-fitted bodice, puffed sleeves, and a full skirt. But, wait, I already have a dress like that. See the section on *Annie Get Your Gun.* It is the dress used for the Town Woman on page 27. By adding an apron made of a woman's nightgown and a mop hat (see page 102), it works for another scene. See Mabel Costume.

All the dresses used can be modeled on Mabel's dress. The nightgowns worn by the girls in another scene can be found easily and cheaply at thrift stores and rummage sales.

Mabel Costume

Mabel
Original Garment

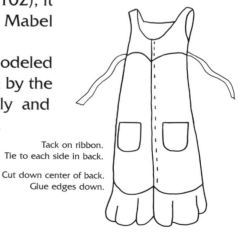

Tack on ribbon.
Tie to each side in back.

Cut down center of back.
Glue edges down.

Speaking of nightwear, the **Major General** is seen in a long, white nightshirt, robe, and nightcap. Using the full-sleeved blouse for the Pirate King, I cut it off below the third button, sewed the full section of a woman's nightgown to the hem, and added a robe. The night cap is made by gluing two pieces of fabric together and turning it right side out. See Major General Costume #2.

The **Sergeant of Police** is the comedian of the production. He wears a British-style bobby costume. To achieve the look, see the East Indian Manservant Costume (page 17) from the section on *Annie.*

If the lab coat and pants were dyed navy blue, and you added a black belt, badge, and a different hat, you would have a British bobby. If you can't find gold buttons, make them of fabric paint directly on the front of the long coat.

To purchase bobby hats, night sticks, and badges, see the reference section.

Major General Costume #2

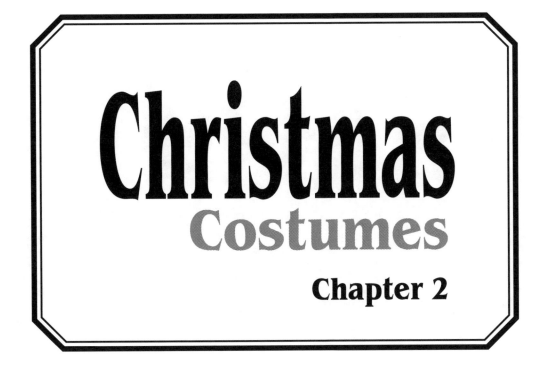

Christmas
Costumes
Chapter 2

The Christmas parade is coming up. You would like to have an entry, but what about the costumes?

You have been asked to be Santa's helper at the annual Christmas party. What will you wear?

You work at a job that requires you to dress up for holidays. Your money is tight—how do you come up with a cheap and easy costume?

Let's start with the parade. You don't have to do a full float if you have a wonderful costume. How would you like to be a walking **Christmas Tree**? See if you can find an old hoop skirt. See Christmas Tree Costume.

Christmas Tree Costume

Christmas Tree
Original Garment

Star

Cut armhole here.

Use opening as one armhole.

Green garland

Ribbon

Glue green garland to cover the hoop skirt. Decorate.

Making the Costume

1. The hoop skirt should have a slit in one side where it ties together. Consider that an armhole. Cut another armhole on the other side and glue the edges down.
2. Remove the boning and dye the hoop skirt with green dye. Replace the boning.
3. Glue green garland all around your hoop skirt to give it a tree appearance.
4. Decorate as you would a Christmas tree, making sure everything is glued or tied on well and is unbreakable.
5. Use posterboard or foam to make a cone-shaped hat. Before you decorate, fasten ribbons or hook and loop tape to the cone to hold it on securely. Decorate to match the tree.
6. Add red and white striped socks or tights (see reference section) and a pair of short white gloves.
7. If you wish, you can light your tree with battery-operated lights.

Santa's helpers come in several forms. You could be **Mrs. Claus**, **Miss Claus**, or an Elf.

As you search the thrift stores, think red and white. I located a woman's long red robe with white piping, bought a high-necked, ruffled blouse with ruffles at the cuffs and added a ruffled white apron over the robe. A Santa hat and a pair of small round glasses complete the costume for Mrs. Claus.

Miss Claus is simply a younger sexier version of Mrs. Claus.

Making the Costume

1. Cut the bottom off the robe.
2. Add white fur trim around the hood, hem, and cuffs.
3. Remove white robe tie and add a black belt.
4. Add Santa hat. If you can't find one, you can cut two pieces of fabric out of the bottom of the dress and glue an edge of fur around it.
5. If you want a more modest look for Miss Claus, you might add red or black tights to the costume.

Miss Claus

Add fur.

Add fur.

Add fur.

Remove tie.
Add belt.

Cut here.

Add fur.

Mrs./Miss Claus
Original Garment

So you want to be an **Elf**. Think red, white, and green. When I went in search of my base clothing for the male elf, I found a pair of green pants, a large woman's green vest, and a full-sleeved blouse with ruffles at the cuff. Perfect for my male elf. See Male Elf Costume.

Making the Costume

1. Cut green pants off just below the knees and glue hem in.
2. Add a white blouse and a green vest.
3. See section on *Peter Pan* (page 91) for how to make the hat.
4. Add red socks and pointed-toe shoes (see reference section).
5. To make the ruffle for the neck, cut a piece of fabric in a "U", glue down the top over a shoestring to tie in back, and glue rows of ruffle to the "U" (see page 79).

Male Elf Costume

Male Elf Costume
Original Garment

For my female elf, I found a stretchy, one-piece red and white outfit. See Female Elf Costume.

Making the Costume

1. Add red and white striped socks and pointed-toe shoes.
2. A leather-like fabric can be used to fashion an apron. Add a shoestring to go around the neck and two more to tie the back together.
3. The collar and hat are made of green felt. Cut the collar in a jagged design. You could sew bells on each point if you wish to jingle. The hat is two pieces glued together and a feather.
4. Add ruffle at the neck and short white gloves for a finished look.

Female Elf Costume

Female Elf Costume
Original Garment

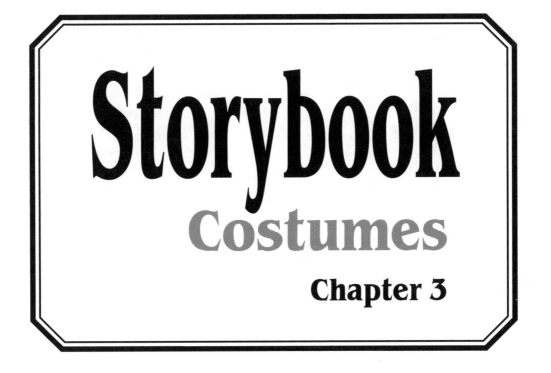

Storybook
Costumes
Chapter 3

As a child, one of my favorite storybook characters was **Peter Pan**. How I longed to fly through the air with him and his group of children. It is a simple enough costume. I would encourage you to seek out a garment that does not fray since you will be cutting the bottom and sleeves jagged and you will not want to hem them. See Peter Pan Costume.

Peter Pan Costume

Making the Costume

1. Dye dress green.
2. Cut the hem and sleeves in a jagged design.
3. Use green glitter fabric paint to enhance the costume.
4. Make a green hat from the bottom of the dress. Cut two pieces from the skirt fabric and glue them together for the hat. Add a feather.
5. A pair of green tights completes the costume.

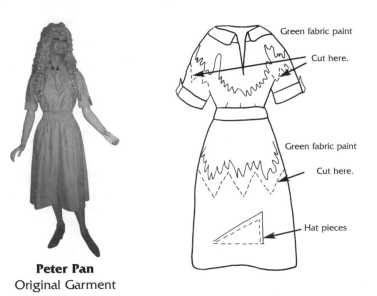

Peter Pan
Original Garment

Green fabric paint

Cut here.

Green fabric paint

Cut here.

Hat pieces

Every good story needs a villain. **Captain Hook** is the villain, and a flashy one at that. He wears a great black and red pirate costume and a big mustache to make him appear evil. See Captain Hook Costume.

Captain Hook Costume

Making the Costume

1. Start with a man's black overcoat. Remove any buttons. Fold front lapels under and glue, making sure it separates more in the lower front.
2. I used the red satin fabric left over from the underskirt of Dolly's dress (See page 51) for the front lapels and cuffs. Glue wide strips of red fabric down both sides of the front.
3. Glue buttons on and decorate with gold fabric paint.
4. Stand the collar up, glue red satin fabric over and inside the collar and glue buttons on. Decorate with fabric paint.
5. Add a pair of women's satin, blousy pants and boot tops. (See pattern for boot tops in the *Pirates of Penzance* section, page 79.)
6. The undervest, mock sash belt, and neck ruffle are from the Pirate King in the *Pirates of Penzance* section (page 79).
7. The hook is made from twisted aluminum foil and shaped into a hook.

Captain Hook
Original Garment

Captain Hook
Original Garment

Cut pants off above elastic. Release sheer overdress at waist.

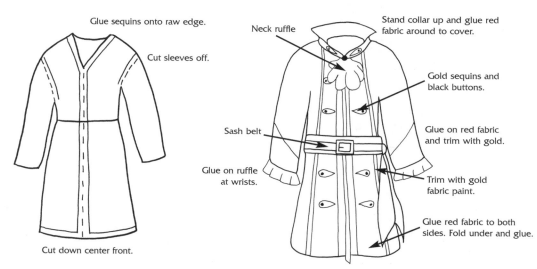

Glue sequins onto raw edge.

Cut sleeves off.

Cut down center front.

Neck ruffle

Stand collar up and glue red fabric around to cover.

Gold sequins and black buttons.

Sash belt

Glue on red fabric and trim with gold.

Glue on ruffle at wrists.

Trim with gold fabric paint.

Glue red fabric to both sides. Fold under and glue.

These costumes make a good couples set for Halloween. They can be used in a production of *Peter Pan*, or they are fine used singly.

Although there are many storybook characters you may do costumes for, I will only do a couple more to give you the idea. They are wonderful to use in plays, parades, for children's programs, and any other occasions requiring you to dress like a character from a storybook. I used to do costumes for a lady from the library who would dress according to whatever story she was reading to the children. It helped get their attention.

Little Miss Muffett sat on her tuffet in a really cute outfit. See Little Miss Muffett Costume.

Little Miss Muffett Costume

Making the Costume

1. Remove the underlayer of the skirt at the waist, just below the zipper.
2. With two safety pins, bring the dress up from the tops of the gathers to the waist. Pin to the waist and glue flowers over pins. Repeat in back.
3. Put a high-necked white blouse with a neck ruffle under the dress.
4. Add a belt, a mop hat made from the small satin muff, and a novelty spider.

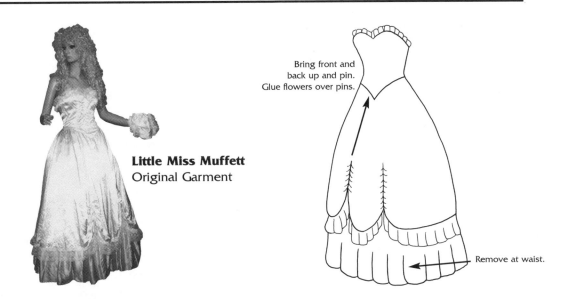

Little Miss Muffett
Original Garment

Bring front and back up and pin. Glue flowers over pins.

Remove at waist.

If the dress is too short, don't go up as high when you pin it. It will still look good. However, if you would like a more sexy Miss Muffett, wear the dress without the blouse. The choice is yours.

Pinocchio Costume

Pinocchio was a wooden puppet, suddenly transformed into a real boy. All the children know this costume. See Pinocchio Costume.

Making the Costume

1. Buy a pair of women's red pants with an elastic waist.
2. Hem just above the knee.
3. Add red suspenders and glue on large white buttons where the suspenders fasten to the pants.
4. A yellow short-sleeved shirt, black vest and white gloves finish the costume.
5. I spray-painted a man's hat yellow and added a black hatband and a red feather. A piece of blue fabric was tied into a bow at the neck.
6. A pair of men's long white socks and a pair of gold house slippers were added.

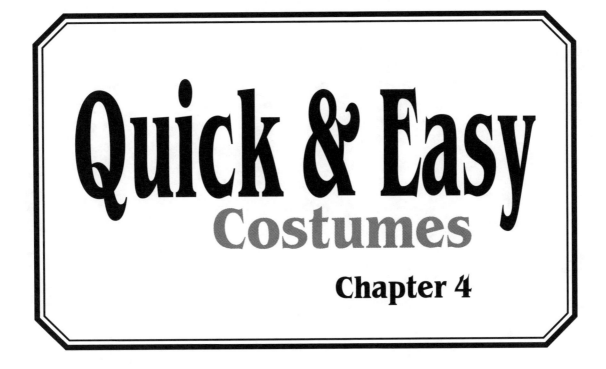

On my journeys through thrift stores, antique shops, and rummage sales, I have found many items with potential that were not used for my theatrical costumes. I decided that rather than waste them, I would use them to show you how to make quick, easy, inexpensive costumes.

Many of the costumes in this chapter are "throw togethers" and could be worn for theme nights, Halloween, and even for plays. Many times a costume is not a matter of sewing and designing, but looking for the right pieces that fit together and give you the look you desire.

Just because a costume doesn't take sewing, time, or expertise, does not mean it is not a good costume. See what you think.

Princess Costume

Everyone wants to be a **Princess**. I purchased the white dress with a pink ribbon belt in a group of garments. The dress cost me around eight dollars. Underneath the long, lace overlay skirt were layers of white chiffon. What a find. See Princess Costume.

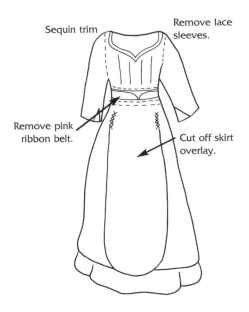

Making the Costume

1. Remove the ribbon belt. Carefully cut the lace overskirt off at the waist.
2. Remove sleeves.
3. Glue silver sequins at bodice top, down the bodice, and at the waist.
4. Tiara is made of pipe cleaners with fabric paint.
5. Add jewelry and long gloves.

Sequin trim

Remove lace sleeves.

Remove pink ribbon belt.

Cut off skirt overlay.

Princess Costume
Original Garment

The Princess Costume could be used for the production *Evita*. It would make a great gown for the lead.

Prince Costume

If you have a Princess, you will need a **Prince**. That can be a daunting proposition if you don't keep it simple. A prince costume could be used in any number of ways. He could be in a production of *Cinderella*, a complement costume for the Princess at Halloween, or perhaps on a theme float.

I've put together the most simple Prince I could think of without losing elegance. This is the same costume used for Frederick in the section on Pirates of Penzance on page 79. The only difference is the accessories. I bought a beret and glued feathers on, with a piece of jewelry to cover the area where I had glued. See Prince Costume.

Medieval Lady Costume

I'm sure you will see that same old long black dress that is at many rummage sales and inevitably in the thrift shops. It is made of a nylon mixed fabric and just hangs there. You can usually purchase them cheap because no one wants them — except costumers.

One of the theatrical productions I'd thought of doing was *Macbeth*. I saw this black dress and knew it would be wonderful for Lady Macbeth. I didn't do the play, but I did do the costume. I couldn't resist. See **Medieval Lady** Costume.

This dress was fabulous to work with because the fabric does not fray. You could cut the skirt into strips and it would work. Pay attention to the fabric of the garment — it will make building the costume a joy or a terror. This one was fun.

Medieval Lady
Original Garment

Making the Costume

1. Using the short black dress, cut off the skirt, straps, and upper bra. Cut out the back zipper and add hook and loop tape to close.
2. On the long black dress, cut the neck into a V shape. Cut holes in the sides of the chest and on the arms. Glue a V-shaped extension to the cuffs.

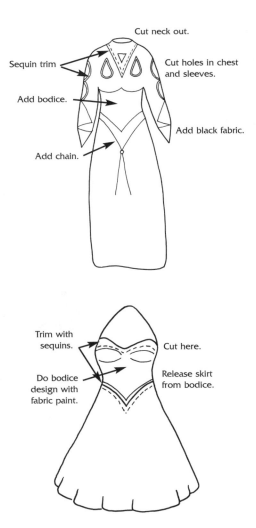

Cut neck out.

Sequin trim

Cut holes in chest and sleeves.

Add bodice.

Add black fabric.

Add chain.

Trim with sequins.

Cut here.

Do bodice design with fabric paint.

Release skirt from bodice.

3. Glue sequin trim at neckline, around holes, and down arms.
4. On what you have left of the short dress, glue sequins around the edges and use fabric paint drops to decorate.
5. I used a long chain necklace to hang down the front of the skirt. It is pinned inside the overdress.
6. The cape was a green skirt. I cut the seam out and fastened the waist corners at the neck with a large brooch.
7. A lightweight chain was added to the forehead for that finished look.

Medieval Lady
Original Garment

What can you make with a tablecloth? I can make any number of things. I found a white tablecloth with silver trim at a church rummage sale. It was a great, heavy, non-fray fabric.

For my first costume, I chose a **Sheik**. By making a slit in one end of the tablecloth, several inches from the hem, I could put it over the head and have a wonderful Arabian cape.

A woman's dressy, split pants would work for the pants. I ran orange shoestrings through the hem of each leg and tied them. It gave me the bloomered pants I needed.

The turban was made by wrapping silver fabric around the dome of a hat and gluing the edges down. I glued two feathers in the front and decorated with gold Christmas beads. A black vest and chain medallion finished the costume.

See Sheik Costume.

Sheik Costume

As I looked at the costume, I realized it would also make a great toga style costume for **Caesar**. By bringing the two corners up and pinning them to the neckline, I had another costume. I added sporadic pieces of hook and loop tape down the front to hold it together. The wig and beard gave it the finished look. See Caesar Costume.

When I removed the beard and wig to undress the mannequin, I saw a **Holy Man**. Yes, with the bald head, the costume took on another look. See Holy Man Costume.

Caesar Costume

So, what can you do with a tablecloth? You can make any number of costumes or costume parts. You are limited only by your imagination. Let it run wild when you are costuming.

Holy Man Costume

Belly Dancer Costume

The strapless purple, black, and white dress was given to me. I could see a **Belly Dancer** as a partner for my Sheik costume. That wonderful skirt would make a fabulous belly dancer skirt. But what about the top? If I removed the mid-section of the dress, the top would fall down. I found a simple solution. See Belly Dancer Costume.

Belly Dancer
Original Garment

Making the Costume

1. Using a front-closure brassiere, cut the bust out of the dress and glue it directly to the cups. Glue sequin trim on to cover the edges.
2. Hanging beads are a good accent for the top. Use lightweight beads and glue them in spots, to hang down over the stomach.

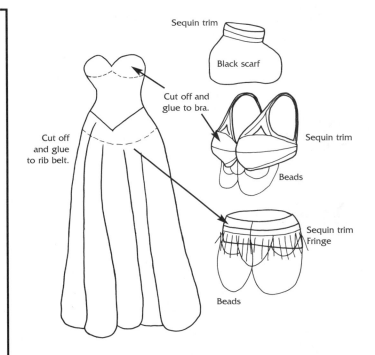

3. Purchase a rib belt. You can buy one in a medical supply store for around nine dollars. Make sure it fits the hips snugly and comfortably without stretching. Once you use glue on it, it will no longer be stretchy.

4. Cut the skirt off the dress. Glue it directly to the lower half of the rib belt.

5. Starting at the place you glued the skirt on, glue on rows of fringe and sequins. Add beads the same as you did to the top.

6. The hat was a woman's pillbox hat. I covered it with sequins and a black scarf to frame the face.

7. Add a shawl if desired.

8. Sandals work well with this costume.

If you are looking for a nice couples costume, the Belly Dancer will work well with the Sheik. You should be a hit at any party.

The **Colonial Man** is a "throw together" costume. I purchased a long vest from the women's plus-size area, added a woman's full-sleeved, extra-large blouse, and cut a pair of sweatpants off for knickers. The neck ruffle I made as before (see page 79). Put a feather in your hat and call yourself a Colonial Man.

If you happen to be doing a production of *1776*, you might be able to use this type of costume. For a coat, see Scrooge Costume #1 in the section on A Christmas Carol (page 37). See Colonial Man Costume.

**Colonial Man
Costume**

**Colonial Woman
Costume**

Colonial Woman
Original Garment

I found a print dress with elbow-length sleeves and a round collar that would work well for a **Colonial Woman.**

Do you remember the ruffled apron I found in the lobby of a country eating establishment? I used it in *Oklahoma!* over a dress. You could modify the apron to make the panniers, and the mop hat can be made from the bib of the apron.

You will need to add a crinoline under the dress. See Colonial Woman Costume.

Colonial Woman
Original Garment

Colonial Woman
Original Garment

Making the Costume

1. Cut up the sides of an underskirt to a V at the waist. Then cut up the sides of the print dress and sew one half of the slip into each side of the dress.
2. Cut the bib off the apron and glue down the edge.
3. Pull center hem up to the waist and pin it from underneath.
4. To make a mop hat, cut a circle out of the bib and glue an edge of lace around it. Go a couple of inches in and stretch sew a piece of thin elastic around the circle. This completes the mop hat.
5. Any type of little stretch slipper will work for shoes.

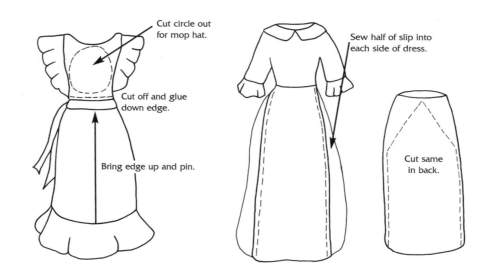

Cut circle out for mop hat.

Cut off and glue down edge.

Bring edge up and pin.

Sew half of slip into each side of dress.

Cut same in back.

Almost any costume can be made to look sexy on a woman. The next four costumes are examples of easy ways to make costumes more appealing to people who like to show a little skin.

Line dancing and western theme parties abound throughout the U.S., and people are always trying to come up with a different kind of **Cowgirl.**

I bought a really ugly pair of leather culottes at a garage sale. Later, I found a leather front vest that was close in color. A torn man's leather coat for fifty cents would make great fringe. See Cowgirl Costume.

This is the only costume in the book that is not washable. It will have to be dry-cleaned because of the leather.

Cowgirl Costume

Cowgirl Costume
Back View

Cowgirl
Original Garment

Making the Costume

1. Back view: Cut the back of the legs out, just below the panty line. Leave enough fabric to make fringe at the panty line.
2. Front view: Glue a section to each leg made from the back legs you cut off. Glue to the hem of the front leg. Round the hem off with scissors to the length you want.
3. Cut strips of leather out of an old coat and glue them to the vest and pants. Be sure you use some where you glued the fabric together to cover it. Fringe strips. Use a thin strip on the back of each leg to hold the chaps in place.
4. Use drops of fabric paint to give it that beaded look.
5. Add a hat, jewelry, and guns. See reference section for toy guns.

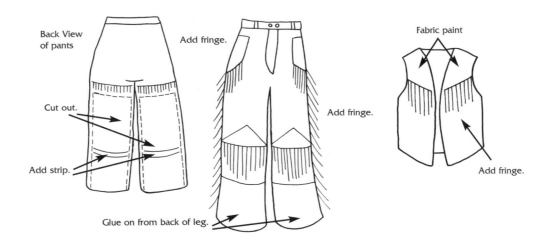

Devil Costume

Devil Costume
Original Garment

Another sexy costume that is easy to make is a **Devil**. Just because you are a devil, doesn't mean you have to be ugly or all covered up. Almost any red dress will work for a devil costume with a little imagination, a pair of scissors, and some glue. I found a straight-line red dress for my devil. See Devil Costume.

Making the Costume

1. Red dress, non-fray fabric: Begin at the hip and fringe dress at an angle.
2. Fringe the sleeves.
3. Cut a diamond-shaped hole in the upper bodice. Glue a sheer black net fabric over the hole. Trim the edges off. Glue sequin trim to cover the edges.
4. I made pitchfork designs on the hip and chest out of drops of gold glitter fabric paint.
5. Add a tie sash belt with the tail attached, a short black cape, and a set of horns. I used fishnet hose for my devil.

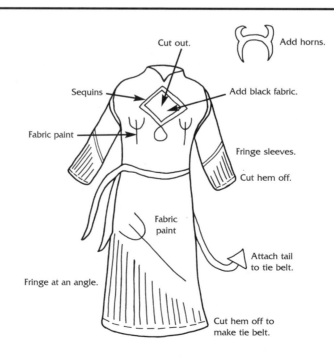

Witches can be fun. They are easy to wear, cool, and, if you make a sexy one, can be quite attractive. See Witch Costume.

Witch Costume
Original Garment

Making the Costume

1. Black, non-fray dress: Cut the skirt off just above the elastic waist. Cut the hem in a jagged line.
2. Place the skirt over the top, with panty attached. Add a wide metal belt to cover waist.
3. Add a witch's hat, a short cape, and jewelry.

Witch Costume

Witch Costume
Original Garment

"I would like something sexy and easy to wear but I really don't want much skin to show." How many times have I heard that?

My **Asian Woman Costume** might fit the bill. She is completely covered, with just a hint of skin showing through the slit in the front of the dress; and yet, somehow, still sexy. See Asian Woman Costume.

Asian Woman Costume

Making the Costume

1. Remove the zipper and collar from the red graduation gown.
2. Remove the belt from the silver dress. Split it lengthwise.

Asian Woman
Original Garment

3. Glue half of the belt to each sleeve of the graduation gown.
4. Glue gold and black trim around the edges of the graduation gown.
5. Glue gold and black trim at waist, across the front, and around the neck of the silver dress. Decorate with fabric paint.
6. The cone-shaped hat can be made from posterboard, covered with silver fabric on the underside and with red fabric on the outside. Glue a piece of a black feather boa at the crown and trim edge with gold trim.

Asian Woman
Original Garment

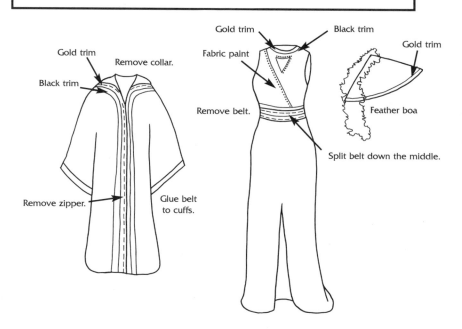

**Girlie Boy
Costume**

Many of my male customers want to dress like women for a joke or for Halloween. They don't want to be just a woman, but they usually want to be sexy and funny. You can look for large-sized dresses to fit them or you could go with a different look. I chose the more unusual of the two. See **Girlie Boy** Costume.

Girlie Boy is not only the sexy look they want, but with the right mask, it is funny. People enjoy funny costumes.

Girlie Boy
Original Garment

Making the Costume

1. Double-ruffled, black and white polka-dotted skirt with elastic waist: Cut the lower ruffle off, above the gathers, inside the skirt.
2. Add hook and loop tape to hold it together. It will be worn over one shoulder and under the other arm.
3. Cut the waist off the black, non-fray skirt.
4. Sew the black skirt inside the ruffled skirt, where you removed the lower ruffle.
5. Cut a section out of the center front of the black skirt so the legs will show.
6. Add black fishnet hose, a feather boa, a woman's half mask, and a blond curly wig.

Girlie Boy
Original Garment

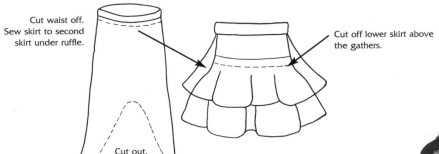

Cut waist off.
Sew skirt to second
skirt under ruffle.

Cut off lower skirt above
the gathers.

Cut out.

You don't have to do much to make a funny costume with very little money. I bought a great woman's mask at an after-Halloween sale at one of the big discount stores. The wig was a part of the mask, so I didn't have to worry about hair. See **Bag Bertha** Costume.

If she doesn't make you laugh, you need your sense of humor realigned.

Bag Bertha Costume
Front view

Bag Bertha Costume
Back view

Making the Costume

1. Stuff an old one-piece corset with fiber fill.
2. Decorate a black stretch blouse with rhinestones and fabric paint.
3. Add striped stretchy pants, a big belt, purse and bag. The hat is the brim of an old witch's hat. The big bag is one I had at the house.
4. I glued rhinestones onto sunglasses and added gold high heels.

Bag Bertha
Original Garment

Clown Costume Original Garments

Cut here.

Glue skirt to legs.

Clowns are always fun. What? You say you can't do makeup? Well, with this costume, you don't have to.

I bought a pair of men's bright yellow pants and a red shirt at a thrift store. The short red dress was from a rummage sale and would make up the ruffles for the pants. The large ruffle for the neck was the same ruffle I used for Girlie Boy's costume top. I wrapped it around twice.

Add white gloves, a funny half mask, a tall striped hat, and big plastic feet that will fit over your shoes. For the accessories you can't find, see the reference section at the back of the book. See Clown Costume.

Clown Costume

Clown Costume
Original Garment

The next fifteen costumes are all "Throw Togethers" that need only to be hemmed or a little garnish added. I will list them in the order in which they will appear.

1. 1920s Newsboy
2. Gibson Girl
3. 1920s Gay Blade
4. 1920s Female Swimwear
5. Beachcomber
6. Hula Woman
7. Hula Woman for larger sizes
8. Greaser
9. Poodle Skirt for Pink Lady
10. Red Poodle Skirt
11. Yachtsman
12. The Phantom
13. Count Dracula
14. Mime or Mardi Gras Man
15. Wolfman

1. 1920s Newsboy

2. Gibson Girl

3. 1920s Gay Blade

4. 1920s Female Swimwear

5. Beachcomber

7. Hula Woman for larger sizes
(Your Author)

6. Hula Woman

All the costumes above were purchased as used clothing, except for the black leather jacket, which I retrieved from a friend who used to be into motorcycles.

The poodle skirts are a matter of gluing a poodle on and adding a crinoline.

If you own an old tuxedo or know someone who does, The Phantom and Count Dracula are easy to put together.

The rest of the costumes are pretty self-explanatory. Pay attention to the details and your costumes will come together well.

I hope that I have covered a large enough range of costumes in this book so that you will be able to find whatever you need and figure out a way to convert it into a costume. Always remember and never forget, "Whatever works!" and "Never sew if you don't have to."

8. Greaser

**9. Poodle Skirt
for Pink Lady**

10. Red Poodle Skirt

**14. Mime or
Mardi Gras Man**

15. Wolfman

11. Yachtsman

12. The Phantom

13. Count Dracula

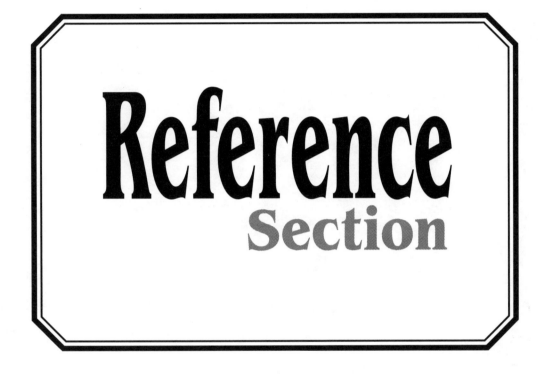

References

Caufields 1006 W. Main St. Louisville, KY 40202 1-800-777-5653	Costumes, Accessories
Junk for Joy P.O. Box 93039 Los Angeles, CA 90093 (213) 856-9560 (818) 569-4903	Vintage clothes, shoes, hats, costume accessories
Rubie's Costumes One Rubie Plaza Richmond Hills, NY 11418 (718) 739-4040	Costumes, accessories, makeup
Morris Costumes 3108 Monroe Rd. Charlotte, NC 28205 (704) 332-3304 1-800-334-4678	Costumes, accessories, masks, props
Oriental Trading 4206 S. 108th St. Omaha, NE 68137 (402) 331-5511 1-800-226-2269	Costume accessories
Zucker Feather Products 512 N. East St., Box 289 California, MO 56018 (314) 796-2183 1-800-443-6786	Feathers and feather trim

Hatcrafters 4th and Main, Box 266 Betterton, MD 21610 (215) 623-2620	Over 400 styles of hats in felt and straw, better hats and more expensive
Lacy Fashion Wigs 249 W. 30th St., Suite 707 New York, NY 10001 (212) 695-1996 1-800-562-9911	Costume character and theatrical wigs
Masters Tuxedos 3600 Market Youngstown, OH 44507 (216) 788-9932	Formal wear, new and dyed; period wear for men
Sweetheart Slips P.O. Box 69-3793 Miami, FL 33269-0793 (305) 653-1616 1-800-227-7547	All types of women's slips
Magique Novelties 240 Westgate Carol Stream, IL 60188 (708) 653-7712	Costume accessories, props
Eddie's Trick Shop 262 Rio Circle Decatur, GA 30030 (404) 377-0003 1-800-544-8278	Makeup, clown supplies, wigs, masks, costumes, props
Sculptural Arts Coating, Inc. P.O. Box 13113 Greensboro, NC 27415 (910) 299-5755 1-800-743-0379	Sculpt or coat

Red Hill Adhesives
P.O. Box 4234
Gettysburg, PA 17325
(717) 337-3038
1-800-822-4003

Glue guns and glue

About the Author

A single mother for many years, Barb Rogers haunted thrift shops, rummage sales, and auctions in the hope of finding old clothes that could be converted into costumes and sold. Not a seamstress, unable to use a pattern, and without a sewing machine, she developed her own unique way of designing costumes.

After returning to school, she completed a Bachelor's Degree from Eastern Illinois University, where she studied psychology and communications, but her first love remained costuming.

Broadway Bazaar Costumes was born in one upstairs room, on the main street of Mattoon, Illinois, with 130 costumes, and her burning desire to succeed. Within five years, it had grown to fifteen rooms of fun, fabulous, flamboyant costumes.

A member of the National Costumers Association, Barb attended national conventions, competed with costumers from all over the U.S., and won many awards. But after ten years in business, she was brought down by a serious illness.

Always the survivor and eternal optimist, but unable to continue running the shop, she leased it out and found her second love: writing. Barb and her husband, Junior, and two dogs, Sammi and Georgie, relocated to a small mountain community in Arizona, where she could heal and write. Since that time, in addition to working on her costuming books, Barb has written a murder mystery, two romance novels, and two inspirational novels.

At age fifty-one, Barb hopes to become a published novelist, but will always hold on to her first love: costuming.

Order Form

Meriwether Publishing, Ltd.
P.O. Box 7710
Colorado Springs, CO 80933
Telephone: (719) 594-4422
Website: www.meriwetherpublishing.com

Please send me the following books:

_____ **Costuming Made Easy #BK-B229**   **$19.95**
by Barb Rogers
How to make theatrical costumes from cast-off clothing

_____ **Elegantly Frugal Costumes #BK-B125**   **$14.95**
by Shirley Dearing
A do-it-yourself costume maker's guide

_____ **Broadway Costumes on a Budget #BK-B166** **$14.95**
by Janet Litherland and Sue McAnally
Big-time ideas for amateur producers

_____ **Costuming the Christmas and Easter**   **$10.95**
Play #BK-B180
by Alice M. Staeheli
How to costume any religious play

_____ **Self-Supporting Scenery #BK-B105**   **$15.95**
by James Hull Miller
A scenic workbook for the open stage

_____ **Stage Lighting in the Boondocks #BK-B141** **$12.95**
by James Hull Miller
A simplified guide to stage lighting

_____ **Everything About Theatre! #BK-B200**   **$16.95**
by Robert L. Lee
The guidebook of theatre fundamentals

These and other fine Meriwether Publishing books are available at your local bookstore or direct from the publisher. Use the handy order form on this page.

Name: _____

Organization name: _____

Address: _____

City: _____ State: _____

Zip: _____ Phone: _____

❑ **Check Enclosed**
❑ **Visa or MasterCard #** _____

                                        Expiration
Signature: _____ Date: _____
        (required for Visa/MasterCard orders)

Colorado Residents: Please add 3% sales tax.
Shipping: Include $2.75 for the first book and 50¢ for each additional book ordered.

❑ *Please send me a copy of your complete catalog of books and plays.*

Order Form

Meriwether Publishing, Ltd.
P.O. Box 7710
Colorado Springs, CO 80933
Telephone: (719) 594-4422
Website: www.meriwetherpublishing.com

Please send me the following books:

_____ **Costuming Made Easy #BK-B229**   **$19.95**
by Barb Rogers
How to make theatrical costumes from cast-off clothing

_____ **Elegantly Frugal Costumes #BK-B125**   **$14.95**
by Shirley Dearing
A do-it-yourself costume maker's guide

_____ **Broadway Costumes on a Budget #BK-B166**   **$14.95**
by Janet Litherland and Sue McAnally
Big-time ideas for amateur producers

_____ **Costuming the Christmas and Easter**   **$10.95**
Play #BK-B180
by Alice M. Staeheli
How to costume any religious play

_____ **Self-Supporting Scenery #BK-B105**   **$15.95**
by James Hull Miller
A scenic workbook for the open stage

_____ **Stage Lighting in the Boondocks #BK-B141**   **$12.95**
by James Hull Miller
A simplified guide to stage lighting

_____ **Everything About Theatre! #BK-B200**   **$16.95**
by Robert L. Lee
The guidebook of theatre fundamentals

These and other fine Meriwether Publishing books are available at your local bookstore or direct from the publisher. Use the handy order form on this page.

Name:_____

Organization name: _____

Address: _____

City: _____ State:_____

Zip: _____ Phone: _____
   ❑ **Check Enclosed**
   ❑ **Visa or MasterCard #** _____

Signature: _____   Expiration
                                     Date: _____
    (required for Visa/MasterCard orders)

Colorado Residents: Please add 3% sales tax.
Shipping: Include $2.75 for the first book and 50¢ for each additional book ordered.

   ❑ *Please send me a copy of your complete catalog of books and plays.*